Unbound
Allegiance

Finding Freedom in a
Truth of Your Own

Amy M. Kunkle

DEDICATION

To my children who have been so patient with me
through the process of my awakening and now
writing about it. You are amazing, my beloved
teachers, and I love you with all of my heart.

To my husband, I offer my love and appreciation
for the journey we have been on. Thank you.

To my parents and siblings, you are my soul
mates and I am so happy to be on this planet,
experiencing life with you, I love you and thank
you for your love in return.

Amy M. Kunkle

ACKNOWLEDGMENTS

"You are the average of the five people you spend the most time with." ~ Jim Rohn

During my awakening journey, I was spending the most time with influencers and podcasters, virtually. Some of whom I have never even met, but I appreciate them nonetheless. There are more than five, for anyone counting.

Thank you Jess Lively, Gary Vaynerchuk, Lewis Howes, Aubrey Marcus, Rob Bell, Rich Roll and Julie Piatt.

CONTENTS

Amy M. Kunkle

Unbound Allegiance

Amy M. Kunkle

0

Start Here

Let me say a bit about this book before we get started, because that seems appropriate. I am not a person who reads introductions, so I will not write an introduction. However, I do want you to know why I wrote this book and why you should read it.

This book is about my awakening, plain and simple. There are thousands, perhaps millions of people who are waking up right now. Maybe it's because of the internet, I am not certain, but I do know the consciousness of mankind elevating. That may be a bit dramatic, but I want to acknowledge this isn't just about me, but I am happy to be part of it. People everywhere are looking in the mirror and considering that there may be more to the story than we have been told, or have discovered on our own. It's marvelous, and I am thrilled to be part of this time in history.

This book covers the two years surrounding my awakening, the actual catalyst for my waking up and then the aftermath, which is probably the more interesting part. As much as I have fought internally about this book being about religion, it seems that many things in our culture are built upon that framework. It was the lens with which I viewed the world, and consequently, it is the perspective I leave behind on this journey.

You see, I was raised in a traditional Christian paradigm. I realize most people call it a religion, and not a paradigm. Christianity was a model of how my life was to be lived, it wasn't just a church we went to on Sundays. It started out as just a place we went on Sundays, but as I grew and my life expanded, it became more. My life was based on this model, that someone else created for me. I don't know who "made" the Christian religion, but it surely wasn't Jesus.

In fact, much of Western civilization identifies

with some part of the Jesus story, so it wasn't just me. Heaven and hell, what happens after this life, many of our holidays, marriage, all of these ideas have stemmed from a version of this story. Even if you didn't practice a Christian faith, you probably grew up with some part of the "Jesus" narrative as the basis for your value system. Those values, or allegiances, grew from that starting place.

I spent nearly forty years in the Christian faith, seventeen in a marriage founded on Biblical principles, fifteen of those years raising my children in a Godly way, and then my awakening happened and everything changed. It was like I had been looking at the world in black and white and then all of a sudden everything turned to color. When I started to ask questions, I didn't resonate with the answers.

This book is the journey to find new answers, but not in a paradigm or a system created by culture. The answers had to be found inside of me. And the answers have to be found in you as well. I wrote this book to show the way, and to help you envision how change is possible. But how does that happen? You have to dig deep, stop listening to the world and start listening to yourself. I hope through this book I can help you to discover how to do that, and how to become whole, as Carl Jung, father of analytical psychology, says.

Western religion and culture promise salvation, but we don't need salvation. We need freedom. It's in finding the answers inside yourself that will break you free.

1

The American Dream

I spent my middle and high school years in rural Wisconsin, as if there is another kind of Wisconsin. We moved around a lot, mostly in the Midwest, and always in small towns. I lived in the kind of place that had a population sign prominently displayed at the edge of town. I don't know if you know this, but the census, like in Biblical times, was when they counted everyone everywhere. It happened every ten years, and it was a big deal for our small town when the number changed on the sign. It seemed like it had been 612 forever.

This was the type of town you could imagine is

where you can live the American dream. You can have a big house, with a white picket fence, and inside mom is making dinner with her apron on. Dad, home from work, is playing in the yard with the kids and dog. Everyone is smiling, it seems so great. But is that the American dream? No, it's the American program.

The American program is a mentality that is engrained in us. Woven in the fabric of everything around us, from Disney movies to commercials on television, church and religion, even in the Declaration of Independence. It is the underlying idea that America is the place where you can achieve wealth and happiness in one nation under God. We don't realize that this undercurrent actually drives our life, our decisions, our motives and is reinforced by the society we live in. We strive for this even unconsciously, and it is encouraged. However, the American dream functions like a program that is installed in us like hardware on a computer. It runs in the background, directing us as we go through life.

It should be called the American dream because people are asleep, snoring their way through life. They are dreaming about what it is supposed to be, in denial of what it is. Dreaming about a world that feels unity, instead of the reality of separateness in government, religion and economic status. People are disconnected and alone. They are watching sports and news networks, sucked into listening to how Taylor Swift doesn't show her belly button while playing a game on their phone that is designed to be as addicting as a slot machine.

Maybe we should tell all the immigrants trying to get into America that to live the American dream means they would actually be checking their freedom at the door. They would have better quality of life living in their village, on their terms and connected to purpose, not unconsciously running the *American Dream* program that is on repeat here in the United States.

I was reacting, conforming and listening to everyone and everything outside of myself, until I had enough awareness to realize it. When I had my awakening, as I'll share in this book, I woke up. I saw how I was running this program unconsciously, and was able to bring this into my awareness, and become free, become whole. I wasn't allowed to pick and choose inside of my religion, which is why my awakening didn't come until I was forty years old. I kept my mind closed to outside influence and allowed other people to tell me how to think, and how to determine my value as a human being, instead of learning to discern on my own. I hope I can help you to have the awareness, choose freedom and listen to your own guidance.

Don't Thank or Blame Your Parents

Our society has been running programs from the government, church, and culture as a whole for hundreds, if not thousands of years. Our parents are no exception, and their parents weren't either. We are all, unconsciously passing down programs from generation to generation. You can call them traditions, or family values, or even personalities, but for this book, I am calling them programs.

Our parents raise us, or someone raises us from birth until we establish our own consciousness, or operating system, which happens around age eleven according to most psychologists. It is the point at which you have much of your psyche formed, including your unconscious beliefs and you start forming preferences. This responsibility becomes yours, even though you don't have that much autonomy at age eleven, the torch has been handed by evolution and you live out your life.

I am saying not to thank or blame your parents because it is not the credit or the fault of a person who was not consciously choosing their experience. If your parents were intentional, great, but my estimation is that's less than ten percent of people. They were most likely unaware of how they were raised by their parents, and they in-turn raised you. They did the best they could, but the outcome is just fate, pure luck or "God's will" that things turned out how they did. Until we bring our own program into awareness, and become conscious of how, why and what we are doing, we are all simply the product our environment.

Bloom Where you are Planted

I don't think of my seed as being planted, it was more scattered. By the time I was thirteen, my family lived in twenty-four different homes in many different cities. All of my five siblings were born in different cities than I was, except that the first and third were both born in the same place, but only because we had looped back around. I am the second born, and I was born in Montana.

I have had a lot of life experience, have lived in dozens of cities as a child and as an adult. I believe our unconscious begins to form along with our personality and preferences, at the time of conception. And from there, we adjust based on our life circumstance. The more challenges you have in life, the move evolved you can be, if you recognize the challenges as opportunities for growth. Embrace your story, learn from it and change for the better. If you haven't experienced much in life, you will grow at a slower rate because you don't have a need to change. Without stimulus, many things will remain the same.

Acknowledging your Need

Before you can change, you need to be able to see your need. There are a lot of similarities to Christianity here, and I'm doing that on purpose. Admit that you are a sinner, and ask Jesus to live in your heart…. Yes, I was raised in the church. And I mean, Catholic schools through sixth grade, and private Christian high school, only missing the two years I spent at public school along the way.

I was married in the Christian non-denominational religion and raised my kids in the church for almost thirteen years. If you were raised in the church, let me hear an Amen! I was a born-again believer until about two and a half years ago, when I realized it wasn't my truth.

When I discuss acknowledging your need, it

refers to realizing you have unconscious tendencies, and at least part of you is running a program passed down from family or picked up from culture. This is a concept it could take years to process, or maybe you will look around and realize it right this very minute, because it just clicked.

But, like with everything, you only see what you want to see. I believe one thing religion does for us, is it keeps us unconscious. Religion makes us think that someone else is steering the bus so we should just sit back and go on the ride. We surrender to God's will, and go through life unconsciously.

Why does it matter if we are conscious or not? People seem to be doing pretty well as they are, right? Wrong. Most of us are pretending to be great online or in church, when in fact we are insecure and unable to be real, even with ourselves. Some days, I don't know who we are kidding. Americans are losing their shit. We are the sickest, most anxious and depressed of all time. And at the same time, the richest, so money, obviously, does not equal happiness.

And you don't have to be a tree-hugger to realize our water supply is become completely contaminated, and that is affecting our ground water and soil. We will have to develop a new way to grow food or our population will take a massive hit and thousands, probably millions will die. Whoa, that went dark really fast, I'm sorry. Sometimes the "Oh my God what are we doing to this beautiful planet" monster comes out.

Regardless, our society will have to evolve to fix some of these global problems. Einstein said, "We cannot solve our problems with the same thinking we used when we created them." We created many of these problems, and it is our responsibility to fix them.

You are Here

One of the things I learned in my awakening was the theory of Spiral Dynamics. I want to start here because I feel like it puts everything into perspective. It is a "You are Here" sticker on the journey of life, and is great for us analytical thinkers. Spiral Dynamics is a psychological model developed by Don Edward Beck, and I am sure you will Google it, but I'm going to give a brief explanation anyway. It is visually represented by what looks like a cyclone, or cone. It's small at the bottom and it expands, as does our consciousness, at the top. The different levels are color coded with beige at the bottom, representing instinctive thinking and coral at the top representing enlightened thinking. To equate it to a human that lived, a caveman would be at bottom, or beige (pre-verbal) and Jesus at the top, coral (enlightened).

For many years, nearly forty, I was fixed in the lower-middle of the consciousness spiral, three levels above the caveman and five below Jesus. The color is blue on the cyclone spiral, and the value system is governed by a higher power and is absolute, and unchanging. Now, post-awakening and two plus years of evolution, I have shifted in how I see the world. I am in a higher consciousness state, two or three levels higher (yellow or turquoise), and my value system is balanced and holistic. It is a wider, more inclusive approach, that is subject to growth and change. No system or person can remain stagnant and still evolve.

I hope you don't see this as a judgment on where you are, as I have been there, judging myself. It is comforting to realize we will evolve if we are open to the possibilities. This consciousness spiral helped me to see the extents of my own awareness, and what is possible for humanity.

Conscious Change

This book is all about how to change, and shift your consciousness, your awareness in order to live the life you are meant to live.

When my parents divorced, my dad had custody of my sister and I, but he was moving to Minnesota and we wanted to stay in Wisconsin. We were involved in a Christian school and I was just about to start ninth grade. We were given the opportunity to live with a retired couple on a farm, so we could stay. We would see our parents and siblings on the weekends, but they basically raised us for those three years.

A couple years ago a friend and I were talking. She asked me if I thought that living there was all a show. I guess she was asking if they faked it with us, created a false reality that looked and felt what a traditional, Christian home, was supposed to be like. Every morning they were up at dawn, doing bible study and making breakfast from scratch. We had a very traditional, Christian upbringing for those three years. As if that's not how they really raised their own five children. She was questioning if they were just going to put on this act or illusion for us while we were there at their house because that was the ideal for how children should be raised.

I thought it was an interesting question. I said maybe. It really doesn't matter to me, if they were faking it, good for them. It was what we needed at the time, and maybe what they needed, too. Our time with them changed the trajectory of our lives. Who knows where or how we would have ended up had it not been for them? It was good for us, and I appreciate that time.

By living with them, it was showing us that we could change our lives, and just like that, consciously change the path we were on and therefore, change the destination. My four younger brothers had a very different path than my sister and I did because of this time we spent with this retired couple.

My brothers didn't have this isolated Christian upbringing that my sister and I had. They grew up choosing their value system from the beginning, for themselves. They may not be conscious of choosing a "value system" but they definitely experienced more challenges and figured things out on their own. Thankfully, years later we were "reunited" and have much love and respect for the journeys we each took to get where we are today.

Home of the Brave, Be Brave

It takes courage to choose a different path, or to create your own path. Going against the grain, to be awake when the world is asleep, to look at your own program and question it. It all takes courage. Every step on this journey has been a mini-awakening for me. And if you are open to it, your life will be a series of mini-awakenings as well.

But it takes courage, you have to be brave. It took courage for me to leave my church, and change my ideas about God and the Universe. Bravery was the only option when faced with questions about what I believe about spirituality, purpose, marriage and parenting.

I was taught, growing up, that choosing to follow Jesus was the narrow path. However, that wasn't my experience. It seemed that the path less traveled was filled with Christians. The actual narrow path just has you on it. You, in all your glory, being brave.

2

False Awakenings

I had only made clothes once before in my life, and that was for my sister's high school graduation. Verna had my sister and I find a pattern, and step by step, she taught us how to make an entire outfit. Mine was a jacket style with a solid, pleated skirt, so 90's. I thought it looked better on the front of the pattern package. My sister's turned out great, I was just proud that I had made it myself from scratch.

Growing up in the Catholic church, my family would always get new Easter outfits and then pose before church for a family photo before the mass. Traditions, it should be noted, when gone unchecked can evolve into programs. Unconscious programs that you don't remember why you are doing them years later.

As a married woman, this was a tradition that I brought into my own family, to buy new outfits, or make your own if you're feeling adventurous, and take the token Easter picture.

I asked for a sewing machine from my grandmother for my wedding. I had used it a few times to make curtains and… yep, just curtains. I thought it would be fun to make my daughter's Easter dresses. And so, this Easter when I had two adorable little girls, around two and five years old, I decided to make their matching dresses instead of buying them.

For some reason, I am always drawn to the fanciest fabrics. I picked out a floral sheer organza and proceeded to design my own dresses for them. I was an architect so putting together a dress was something I could handle. However, the organza was not cooperating, hemming it was nearly impossible. What I wouldn't have given for a serger at that moment.

The dresses were created out of white fabric and then sewed the sheer over the top. I was draping it in most cases just securing it with a couple stitches so it would give. And give it did. When we picked the girls up from childcare at church, the dresses were coming apart along the seams. I was trying so hard to make everything perfect, not just on this Easter Sunday, but every day. And instead, things were falling apart at the seams.

Thirty-five

It was Easter 2011, or Resurrection Sunday, as we called it to differentiate ourselves from the other, not as spiritual churches. We had all the things: the matching outfits, the church service, the family photo, and late in the afternoon, stuffed from the large meal that I cooked for my family, I just needed to get out. I changed into exercise clothes and went for a run.

What was wrong with me? I thought half out loud and half inside my head. My life probably looked great to outsiders, but it was so far from perfect. I was in a marriage but felt so disconnected from my husband. I choose to be home raising my children but felt unfulfilled most days. It was never the right time to design and build our own home even though this conversation happened all the time. My husband had recently cancelled our ten year anniversary trip to Australia, it was selfish of us to spend that kind of time and money on a trip. And I turned thirty-five in January, to top it all off.

I needed more than a run.

Running wasn't something I had really done before, but I thought I could probably take better care of myself, Lord knows I wasn't getting any younger. It was a great new habit to clear my head and I was able to get into pretty good shape. But I still needed something to change, I needed to figure out what "this" was.

Getting Advice

During that summer, I took the kids back to visit family in Wisconsin and Minnesota. My mom flew out and drove the fourteen hour trek with me since my husband had to work. On the drive, I asked my mom about her leaving my dad, as she initiated their divorce. It seemed like she could have been going through the same thing I was going through, she was even thirty-five. After they split, she went back to college and pursued her dream of becoming a registered nurse, and had a new boyfriend.

It had been twenty years since their divorce, so I hoped we could speak freely about it, but it didn't turn out that way. I needed her to tell me there was a lesson she learned or insight from her experience, self-reflection or pros and cons, but she didn't really open up. It seemed she wasn't going to be able to help me here.

It Could Just be Hormones

Still seeking answers, I had lunch with a friend from my former church. She was a trusted woman and Christian mentor, who had been married almost ten years longer than me, but was closer to my age.

I admitted some of the feelings I was having, how I felt my heart was hardening towards my husband and that I was resenting him. This wasn't what I had signed up for, I wanted more out of life and had so much more potential. It seemed like pursuing a career was the only option for my independence but I was pretty sure I didn't want that.

She understood and suggested it may be a hormonal shift I was going through. I don't think she meant menopause, God help me, I was only thirty-five! She said it was like a wave of new energy in my system, and she thought it would pass. It was a wave of new energy alright, and I didn't want it to pass. It was invigorating!

Christian Counseling

I had done Christian counseling in college, and now again as an adult. I seemed to work through my issues from childhood and adolescence but raising kids and marriage was taking a toll. The counselor suggested that working may help me feel more accomplished and get out of the house, so I considered that. I just felt called to be a stay-at-home mom and wanted to raise my children. He also suggested bringing my husband in for a few sessions, but I never did. For some reason, I kept feeling like the problem was me.

This is where my awakened self would have stepped in and pointed out that I was only seeking advice from other Christians. Basically, in line with the idea of finding all your answers to life in the Bible, which is what I was taught to do. But now I realize it's only one perspective.

Women Getting "Ideas"

I was determined to live this life to the fullest. And, this is when I discovered podcasts, and not just Christian podcasts.

A friend told me about a fitness podcast, called the Body Do Over Show. I was astonished at how I was learning things I had never known about my body, physiology and even psychology. I found other podcasts like, The Art of Charm, which had so much about social and relationship dynamics. The Smart Passive Income by Pat Flynn,

Entrepreneurs on Fire, by John Lee Dumas which were serious entrepreneurial podcasts. And Raise Your Hand, Say Yes, by Tiffany Han, which was crazy to me that she could just go on the podcast and rant, for lack of a better word, about saying "Yes!" to life. Sign me up!

I felt a bit guilty of how much I loved listening to podcasts. Almost like back in the mid 1900's where women weren't allowed to read books for fear that they'd start getting "ideas" and have a mind of their own. I was gaining an independence with this knowledge that I had never known before.

I think because I went to such a small school that I never read any of the typical books that people read in high school, like Catcher in the Rye (no clue what that's about). Our school worked out of Paces, which were like little workbooks, that had all the information you needed right in there. No need to even open another book. And yet, that didn't seem strange. I was raised in more of a sheltered environment that I had realized, I never read a book, that wasn't a Christian book, until I was thirty-five. This was unbelievable and slightly embarrassing. My first outside book was Julia Cameron's, The Artist's Way, which is still on my bookshelf today.

I felt like a whole world was opening to me, by listening to podcasts. I really enjoyed hearing other people's life stories or success in business, I gravitated towards the ones on entrepreneurship, which was just starting to pop at this time. I was learning about things that I didn't know existed, a world I basically didn't know existed.

I Became an Entrepreneur

I didn't want to work full-time, and I felt that being an entrepreneur was the answer. I decided to start a home-based business selling paper-crafting products. I still had little kids at home and I didn't think I could do architecture at the moment. I had dabbled in this direct-sales company, in California, and now, in the fall of 2011, I felt like I was poised to launch it as a real business, website, blog and eventually, tutorial videos.

As it turned out, I was quite good at making cards. It was a great combination of my love of scrapbooking and my eye for design. I poured my heart and soul into my paper crafting blog, aka lots of time and energy went into it. I had a good mix of socialization with other women as well as annual trips for conferences, to warm places in the country, that I really enjoyed. I was feeling reinvigorated, personally, and I was seeing hope.

I Worked Even Harder

Two years into my paper-crafting business the IRS still called it a hobby, if you get my drift. I wasn't making any money, and I really wanted it to make some income. In the back of my mind was the fact that I was still architect, and had never really worked as one.

I was approached by a business owner at church who needed some AutoCAD drawing done. So, I started working as an independent contractor for a couple hours a week. It wasn't really architecture, but I was doing technical work using my architectural skills, so that was good enough. I was interacting with industry professionals, using the analytical side of my brain, and making money. It was a good thing.

At night I'd work in my craft studio on my blog content, and during the day, I'd do the architectural work in our home office. This was all around the schedule of the children, all of whom were at school during the day, except for the little one. The kids still had sports and ballet, and church activities, plus keeping up the house or as much as I could. I still seemed to have dinner on the table at 5:30 whether my husband came home for it or not. I have always been a bit of an over-achiever.

Amidst all of this, I started to develop a problem in my throat. I couldn't quite figure it out, but every time I went into my home office and sat down at the computer to work, my throat would tighten. This was reminiscent of an anaphylactic reaction, which I'd known since I was allergic to tree nuts. However, I never had a serious allergic reaction, and this wasn't coming on suddenly. It was puzzling, so I thought I'd better get it checked out.

Anxiety

I explained what was happening to my doctor, assuming it was an allergy to mold or something specifically in the office where I did the architectural work. When given some context, my two jobs, responsibilities at home and with the kids and my husband's travel schedule, she didn't think it was an allergy. She thought it may be anxiety. I was a little taken by surprise. I still pushed for the allergy medicine and scheduled a follow-up two weeks later. The allergy pills did nothing, she was right, it was anxiety.

I had a hard time, psychologically, taking the anxiety medication. Maybe it was my pride, or the stigma around the whole idea of mental health. I felt like I should be able to handle this myself, that it was weak of me to give in. I spent some time in prayer, and reconciled that I just needed a little help to get through the current chaos. I was a little surprised that anti-anxiety medication was the same as depression medication. Seemed ironic, and all too coincidental.

The daily medication made me such a zombie, I hated how I felt being on it. I felt like an actual robot, with no control over what was going on around me. I felt like I was swimming through thick lava, not being able to move very fast or react in any way. The second medication, because there were two, was specifically for panic attack type situations. I was only on these medications for a couple months. I scaled down my work load and was able to reduce the triggers for my anxiety.

Mid-life Crisis

How do I know this five year journey was a false awakening and a mid-life crisis and wasn't a full awakening? It's because the problems never left my mind. I was just rearranging my thoughts, trying different approaches, but still not connecting it deeper lessons. I just kept moving onto the next thing that I hoped would bring the change I was seeking. I never tried to figure out how I got to this point of unhappiness, looking deeper at my behaviors or my value system.

Carl Jung, father of analytical psychology, fancifully named the mid-life crisis the Regressive Restoration of the Persona. Our persona is the view the world has of us, which may include our sexual orientation, our personality, job, marital status, religion. An awakening experience, like an accident or just waking up like I did, is something that can make us question the persona we have created. The regressive restoration is when we do not learn the lesson that our awakening experience is here to teach us, and we go back, or regress, to how we were before. Instead, it should force you to dig deeper within yourself for strength, but more often we retreat and prefer to live unhappy, in the familiar dysfunction.

This false awakening was when the persona I created was no longer working, and began to shatter. Life as I had been living, it wasn't working. I think everyone gets to a place in life like that, where if they are honest, it just stops working. Maybe it's a career or relationship, and you are faced with a change or transition, but also not wanting to repeat the same mistakes that got you to this unhappy or unfulfilled place.

The thing is, unhappiness doesn't always push us enough to get out of the situation and really dig deeper to figure ourselves out. I wasn't there yet, I didn't have enough of a discomfort, so to speak, to really connect the lesson. In some cases it takes a cancer diagnosis, a near death experience, or hitting your proverbial rock bottom. I also didn't have the space I needed mentally, or physically to dig deeper.

Another change was coming for us, another opportunity to move and start over for a time. Would it bring the change I was seeking or more of the same? I'll give you a hint, it triggered my awakening.

Amy M. Kunkle

3

Making Space
July 2016-December 2016

We had gone back and forth for years about taking this assignment. When my husband joined this part of the government, we knew that around the seven or eight year mark *this* would become available. We knew we would get the opportunity to take a temporary assignment to their headquarters in Washington, D.C..

The eighteen-month assignment was promised to be a big financial boost, making a good chunk of change for the time you spend there, as well as a pay increase that would put my husband at the top of his range, permanently. It is also strategically positioned in the career of an special agent to advance him to a supervisor role. It would give him the training needed, and then after that, if he wanted to apply for positions as a supervisor, he would be able to do so.

In my mind, to be honest, I was hoping this would be the financial push we could use to build our own house, sooner than later. When we moved to Canton, we had money to buy land but he kept putting me off. He came up with one excuse after another. "We don't know how long we will be here," then when we found out we would be in Canton permanently, it was, "we don't know if we will come back after the D.C. assignment." Then, when I agreed that we should come back and not try and move to Minnesota, which we discussed several times, it was just too much money.

He said he understood my passion to build my own home, as an architect and as a creative woman, but overrode that decision with his humble, Christian position. More recent discussions came back to me not making any money, so ultimately, the ball was in my court. If I just worked as an architect, we could afford to build our own home. I couldn't argue with him, it just never seemed like the right time.

Expand or Explode

Being busy seems to be a way our culture is strengthening its ego. The image, or persona, that we all identify with is bolstered by how much we do and then talk about it online. We flaunt our busyness and brag about the endless activities. And somehow, I intuitively knew that we needed the space. I was feeling the pressure build in our life, there needed to be a release valve soon or things were gonna blow.

I had recently stepped down from my paper-crafting blog, which had been going through some changes already. My contractual job doing AutoCAD fizzled out after the company decided not to expand. I really wasn't sure what was next for me, but I was burnt out, so I welcomed the break.

We had lived in Washington, D.C. before, earlier in our marriage. About two years in, my husband completed his master's program in Forensic Science, paid for by the Air Force. I was pregnant with our first child, our son, who was born mid-way through the year, at the President's Hospital. Living there again, with the whole family was an exciting idea.

Our kids were in first, third and sixth grade. If we went the summer of 2016, all the kids could leave for the year and come back to the same school. They had sports and school activities, but nothing that wouldn't benefit from a change. Besides, the schools in the D.C. area were all S.T.E.M. schools, and the sports programs were top rated. There was no down-side here.

I felt like our marriage needed this, too. It needed a change of scenery and a reset, of sorts. We were going on fifteen years of marriage and I would venture to say, nearly half of them were spent with him gone. Between working long hours or traveling to conferences and court dates, this is a job he loves, but it was taking its toll on our marriage.

In addition to everything else we had going, we were very involved in our church. He was a Deacon and taught our adult Sunday school class every week. I was on the Mission Board and went on mission trips every year, plus the monthly board meetings. The kids were in all the programs, and our family was part of pretty much anything that went on when the church doors were open. I think that's the joke, right? If the doors were open, we were there.

There was pretty much no choice in the matter, this could be what we needed. We were scheduled to leave on July 18th, 2016. The plan was to take only what we needed for the year and leave the rest in our Canton home. I say year because I only agreed to that much. Coming back in the middle of winter wouldn't be an option, so the hubby would have to stay alone for a bit The government would pay for our D.C. apartment, so we could afford to keep our house while we were away.

It was going to be like an extended vacation for us and an adventure we were embarking on. There was more riding on this year away then I even realized, for better or worse, it all happened for us, as it was intended.

The Avalon

I had the kids and the dog in our 2009 Volkswagen minivan and my husband drove the large U-Haul truck. Washington, D.C. was about 5-1/2 hours East and a little South from Canton, Ohio. We would be living in Arlington, Virginia, which is just outside the District of Columbia.

The apartment was less than half the size of our current home, we went from 2,600 SF to 1,100 SF. It was on the third floor and had a balcony overlooking the back of a Rite Aid. This is exactly what you get when you don't look at the apartments in real life. Our dining room table didn't fit, that would have to go back to Canton. Our girls would share a room, our son had his own room, as he would be thirteen this year.

The Avalon was beautiful. The sparkling pool, outdoor grilling areas and turf for kids to play and run. The huge fitness center and yoga rooms were off the main lobby that could pass for an upscale hotel, for sure. There was an indoor and outdoor play area, which we found was really fun for roller blading and skate boarding.

Buckeye, our chocolate lab, had to learn how to be a city dog. Surprisingly, there were a lot of dogs at the Avalon, and not just little dogs. There was a dog park on the property, as well as a walking path all the way around, approximately a city block.

I think what was most amazing about the year we would spend here is that we didn't have a yard to keep up, or a big house to clean. Also, we wouldn't be having friends over or hosting many guests so I wondered if I could go the entire year with minimal housework. Everything was brand new when we moved in that I did no cleaning for at least the first month. It was magical.

The National Mall

There was something about being on the National Mall that connected to my soul. Maybe it was how small I felt standing on the steps of the Lincoln Memorial. Or the dramatic reflection of the Washington Monument in the expansive pool of water. It evoked the feeling of significance, connection and peace that we all long to feel. I had such appreciation for the person who created that experience for us. You wouldn't think the positioning was important until you stood there, yourself, and saw how perfectly the reflection of the Washington Monument appeared in the water.

On Sundays, you could park for free, and if you got there early, which I did, you could park right next to the Washington Monument. It was about a mile and a half from one to the other, and back. Which was perfect because that was exactly how far I wanted to run.

I spent many Sunday mornings in that place, emotionally and physically. It became a practice, or ritual I needed to maintain balance. It was a very different place during the week, and even on Saturday when rallies and protests happened. 2016 was an election year, and an interesting one at that.

The kids and husband didn't love spending time downtown. The traffic, parking and literally thousands of people, were too much for them. After one or two sightseeing trips, we pretty much stayed on our side of the Potomac.

Program Reset

Don't you always secretly hope that moving will solve all you problems and you'll have an amazing new life even though it's just a different zip code? Yeah, I can relate. However, the same programs run in the background of our lives, whether we are conscious of them or not.

For years I would call my brother-in-law to fix my computer issues. Either I had picked up a virus, or just never quite figured out how to delete the temporary internet files that were bogging down my computer. Defragmenting or whatever he did helped for a while, but eventually I would have to get a new computer.

Moving was like cleaning up the hard drive of a computer, it was a good start, but it wasn't a permanent fix. It didn't take long before we had reverted to the life we had in Ohio. The Target runs and gymnastics, kids busy with friends and activities and everyone binge-watching Netflix.

As my own lack of purpose set in, or sheer curiosity, not sure which, I picked up a part time job in Georgetown. I was smitten with the quaint M Street and came across a boutique paper store that drew me in like a moth to a flame. It was enough to occupy my time a few days each week once the kids were in school, otherwise they may have come home one day to find me drawing hash marks on the walls, counting off days with crayons like in the movie, Castaway.

Not How I Planned It

It wasn't even a month that we'd been in D.C. before my husband had to go to Cleveland for a trial. Then, early September it was a trip to Texas to help on a case. Before long, it felt like he was doing more work out of town than he was doing at his new job. I was under the impression he was working an 8 AM – 5 PM desk job, where he would have no nights and weekends to work, and no travel. He was a supervisor now, I thought they only made budgets and wrote performance reviews, from their desk.

Apparently, he had lots of cases to wrap up from Canton, and then new things had come up that required his expertise, hence the traveling away from D.C. Either way, this was not how I had planned it. It's not like I couldn't handle it alone, unlike the six months we lived in Indiana right before Ohio. That I could not handle. That was insane. Three kids under the age of four, in a small apartment, without my husband, no one should have to endure that.

And yet we do, endure that. I blame the program. The program that my Christian upbringing instilled in me that says a wife is to be submissive. And the one from culture that says I am woman, hear me roar. And the one from Disney, that says one day my prince will come. And the one from my husband that says life isn't fair. It's surprising I have any thoughts of my own with all the thoughts the world puts in my head. I just needed to breathe.

Finding My Center

"Take ten deep breaths and then hold your breath while you do pushups? That sounds impossible," I said into the empty living room. I was listening to The School of Greatness Podcast. Lewis Howes, the host, was interviewing Wim Hof, aka the Ice Man. Wim says you can create a physiological reset of the nervous system using the breath. Breathing oxygenates the body and that increases the alkaline nature of the body, which controls stress, and can prevent sickness.

Wim Hof also talked about teaching children to meditate, because they are still open. Open, teachable, not programmed yet. He referenced a Baltimore school that was implementing "Mindful Moments" at the beginning of the day and they are sending kids to the meditation room instead of detention. I took some tips from the show, and found another podcast on meditation, and gave it a shot.

As a Christian, I had never done any kind of meditation, unless you count praying over a verse in the Bible, which is similar. You focus on the verse, dwelling on the meaning, taking it to heart and pray it for yourself. Unless of course, you believe that the Bible verses shouldn't be applied to our life, just ignore that. But, for me that was basic Christian meditation, if there is such a thing.

Not what I was doing though. I was counting my breaths, because it gave my mind something to do, and sitting with my eyes closed. I could only get to low teens before I found the counting stop and my thoughts come in. So I would start over, and set a timer for ten minutes. Later I found out breath counting meditation is from Zen Buddhism, and it's quite common not be able to count very high.

I was amazed at how balanced and centered I felt after meditation. Besides reducing stress levels, I also heard that you can improve your memory with meditation. Even heal connections in your brain that have been "pruned" for one reason or another. You know that feeling when you walk into a room and forget what you went in there to get? After meditating for a couple weeks, I always remembered what I was going in to get.

I welcomed the break from the incessant thoughts that circled in my mind. All the thoughts I was sure no one else ever had. The self-deprecating, angry, unhealthy thoughts that made me feel even more shameful just for thinking them. My journal was filled with these inner most thoughts, and it wasn't pretty.

Choose or Fate Will

I have a friend whose husband was diagnosed with Cancer about seven years ago. When he was sick, and going through treatment, he was a different person. He was kind, humble, loving and connected more deeply with everyone around him. Thankfully, he got better, and went into remission. However, after getting better, he seemed to revert back to the person he was before. It didn't seem as though this he understood the purpose of the experience. He hasn't realized this was happening for him, to grow from. I don't mean to judge his experience, but it changes our perspective when we embrace an experience like this and go to the root of why it is happening and what we can learn.

The Universe, or God, will give you the situation in your life that you need to grow and evolve. If you don't learn a lesson and pass the level, just like in Super Mario Brothers, you will repeat it. Either consciously open and expand or life will force it on you. I was at the point where my persona was crumbling, I was at my rock bottom. I was waving the white flag.

Amy M. Kunkle

4

Waking Up

I have had this dream before. The scene changes, but the events remain the same.

> I'm lost, and I go back to a familiar place to look for something I have forgotten. Someone attacks me and is holding me so tight. It's hard to breathe. When I escape from the grasp around my mouth, I try to scream for help. Nothing. I try again and no sound comes out. I find a sharp object and stab my assailant, but it's not helping.

Then I wake up.

During my morning pages journaling, I wrote down the dream and my analysis of it. I remembered this dream, but looking back over my journal made me realize when it happened. It occurred for the last time right before going to Washington, D.C.. I didn't usually analyze dreams, but I thought since I had this dream before, it must have some significance.

Carl Jung, psychologist, says that dreams were the unconscious beliefs coming forward into the conscious. He believed it was part of the process of individuation, as he called it, or becoming whole. Carl Jung says the Self, with a capitol "S" is the person as a whole, conscious and unconscious integrated. I will use the word Self, capitol "S" when I am referring to the integrated person.

The unconscious belief I must have uncovered was the sense that I was not being heard. I wasn't talking and being ignored, no, I just wasn't able to get the words out, to speak up for myself. This could definitely be about what was going on right now, but it's not the first time this has shown up in my life. Maybe it was a lesson I didn't learn. I didn't recognize this at the time, only in writing this book did I connect the dots. I'll talk more about this when I discuss healing my shadow in chapter nine.

The Catalyst for my Awakening

I was listening to one of my favorite podcasts, The Lively Show. The host, Jess Lively, was from Michigan but was currently traveling around the world, flowing, as she called it. Jess was having an Eat-Pray-Love experience like Liz Gilbert's when she wrote that book. I remember reading Eat, Pray, Love and feeling like, if only. If only I could pick up and go find myself. I thought I was in too deep, this persona I created had too much riding on it. In retrospect, I believe Liz Gilbert and Jess Lively both discovered their Self, capitol "S," through these journeys. However, I didn't realize I could find my Self, without leaving home.

As Jess shared her journey on the podcast, she also shared topics that she was personally was exploring, like the Law of Attraction, Quantum Physics, Abraham Hicks, reprogramming your mind, with Dr. Joe Dispenza and living in the present moment, with Eckhart Tolle. If you were raised like I was, this was edgy, but I still really liked it. Almost like being glued to a soap opera, knowing how bad it is for you, and not being able to turn it off. It was a guilty pleasure.

I was listening to The Lively Show Episode 185: *The intersection of rational mind and intuitive guidance with Erin Loechner.* Jess was shifting the direction of her podcast to align with her current interests. She started by unpacking the concept of ego versus the intuition. Jess described the ego as a fire hydrant, spewing thoughts out about everything, all the time. The intuition was like a well, water still and calm and when you accessed it, you dug deep in yourself, connecting to your heart or gut, to get it.

She explained the left-brain thinking as rational thinking, or the ego. Jess said we could accept the rational and go beyond it with the right-brain processes that were trans-rational, and intuitive. I don't think she said right-brain, but that was a concept I understood. She explained how Einstein knew how to tap into his intuition, and that's how he completed some of his discoveries. She also had her guest, Erin, ask her questions that she answered from her intuition and not her rational, thinking mind. This is the idea of stopping your thoughts to get quiet, or solitude.

Jess also talked about how negative thoughts create negative cells in our bodies, which can create negative health experiences within our bodies, like disease. This was all because we are made of energy, which I'm sure I knew, but didn't think much about.

Former Christian Pastor

As it turned out, I really resonated with the concept of Spiral Dynamics, and wish I had studied it sooner. It was so important to my journey that I covered in my introduction, so go back and get the summary if you missed it. Jess said she learned about Spiral Dynamics from Rob Bell, and though I had heard of him, I was surprised that he was connected with a scientific concept. I underestimated Rob Bell, thinking he was *just* a former Christian pastor. Oh, if he reads this book I hope that makes him laugh.

I started listening to Rob Bell's podcast, which I am confident was the right choice. I identified with his experience, as someone else who also had a traditional Christian backstory. And I saw a model of what life outside the church could look like. It was the virtual influence of Rob Bell's podcast that gave me the courage to write this book, and share my journey. Namaste and thank you Rob Bell.

I feel a bit silly saying that the catalyst in my spiritual awakening was a podcast, but it was. I'm thankful it wasn't a near death experience or a cancer diagnosis. Those are all very real catalysts that can wake people up, and give them a jolt to "Live like You Were Dying" as Tim McGraw says.

This was disrupting my psyche in a whole new way.

Disruption of the Program

I thought, "If we are made of energy, why did Jesus die on the cross for us?" And the whole thing started to unravel. These new ideas of energy and intuition were really challenging the perspective that I held my entire life.

If you are reading this and weren't raised in a Christian or Catholic home, your thoughts may not immediately go to Jesus dying on the cross or what happens after we die. But I couldn't help but wonder if there would even be a need for heaven or hell if we were made of energy? If energy is neither created nor destroyed, Newton's law, not mine, maybe we don't die and go to heaven or hell. Our soul is not destroyed when we die, it's just changed back to spirit, the energy of our soul transitions back into, dare I say, God?

I was like a caterpillar holding onto a branch, getting ready to hang upside down. I wasn't sure what was coming next but I knew I was exactly where I was supposed to be and I had faith that I would be able to figure it out as I went along. This was just the beginning, and this moment shall forever be referred to as my awakening.

Free Will

I remember a song in youth group that went something like this, "There is one way, under heaven by which we must be saved." All the other people or religions who said there are many paths to God were wrong, and our way was right, there is one way and it is through salvation in Jesus Christ. And you closed your mind to any other information. Closed your mind, didn't listen, didn't consider. But isn't free will about choice?

How do we have free will if we only have one side of the argument? If there is one way to Heaven and not, here are the choices, pick one. Or here are a couple of options to consider about the afterlife, choose one. No, that wasn't how I was raised. In fact, if we are all running programs in our minds with predetermined options, the choice isn't really a choice. You don't know the options available that are out of your awareness.

I wanted to choose for myself, with all the information, or at least a lot more information than I've had in the past. I finally felt connected to what I was learning, almost like I worked for it somehow, probably because I did! It felt genuine and authentic, but I still had so many questions.

Quantum Physics

Did God create the world in seven days? This wasn't exactly a physics question, although it kept coming up at my tutoring sessions. As architecture students we needed a basic understanding of how gravity worked, and as it turned out, it was complicated. I wasn't going to make it through physics without a tutor.

Every week we would meet to work through problems, and the conversation seemed to find its way to if the Bible was literal or figurative. Was the world was created in seven, twenty-four hour, days? My rationale always seemed to land on the fact that I believed that God created the world in such a way that we would be able to figure out how he did it, or how it was made. So, if he created the world in seven days, we would be able to figure out some way to explain how he did it. Enter Quantum Physics.

I discovered Quantum Physics during my awakening process, nearly twenty years after that college class. It is the study of sub-atomic particles, and it demonstrates that our words and focus directly influence the particles of matter. Presto!

Speak and create something from nothing. Maybe God used Quantum Physics.

The morale of the story, I didn't have all the answers right then, simply because I didn't have all the questions. But eventually the questions came, and the answers followed.

Sure, I Could Have Ignored It

In an age of information, ignorance is a choice. I heard that statement from Dr. Joe Dispenza, though I do not know if he was the originator. You see, there is so much information online now that no one knows where half of it comes from!

As an architect, many people call me to discuss designing their new home. We talk for a while, I may even stop out to look at a property they want to purchase, and toss around a couple of ideas. More often than not, they come to the decision that there are too many options and they can't envision it, so it is too scary to build a custom home. So, instead, they go to a development, where they get a few different floor pans to choose from to build a home that looks like countless others. They choose to stay within the confines, or comfort zone of an established norm.

It takes vision, imagination and a little bit of

courage to build a home 'from scratch.' But the satisfaction of creating something of their own, and making decisions based on their own values will far outweigh the result they will get in a development.

Staying in your comfort zone will never allow you to reach your full potential. Alignment and freedom far outweigh conforming. Sure, you can be just like everyone else, then you will never know what it feels like to be like you.

5

Fading to Black
January - June 2017

At first, it seemed like my awakening was only affecting my religious beliefs. However, it was deeper than that, because my entire life was anchored on my religious beliefs. This would be a drastic shift in my spirituality, parenting, marriage, health, career and even my personality. There wasn't an area of my life that was left intact. I was experiencing what Carl Jung called Solitio, the disillusion of my ego, my belief system, to make way for a more authentic Self.

Everything was fading to black. Just like when

a butterfly is forming, the caterpillar dissolves completely to make this transition. Somehow it has an energetic pull, by way of an unconscious operating system, that transforms it into the butterfly. I knew I was on the path of transformation and to get there I was in the dark, trusting my own internal guidance system.

Creating Your Own Reality

The idea of creating your own reality was new to me. My exposure to this idea came from two places, Esther Hicks, who channels Abraham, a non-physical entity. Which may be off your woo-woo scale, but it was part of my journey so I'm including it here. The second person was Dr. Joe Dispenza, who shares it from a more scientific approach. I will cover the scientific stuff in a later chapter on energy.

What appealed to me about Esther and Abraham's approach is that it was like motivational speaking from an enlightened perspective. They shared practical ideas about mindset, happiness, relationships, money, meditation, and more. I especially liked how Esther Hicks would talk about wanting more, or being selfish, and manifesting.

My entire life, I have always wanted more, and

for most of that time, I felt shame and guilt for feeling that way. The church, at least the one I attended, taught that I was a sinner and deserved death for my sin. Having everything I want in life was selfish. My husband always said I am never happy with what I have, and I always want more. Esther Hicks and Abraham say that's a good thing!

When Esther and Abraham talked about abundance or selfishness, they said it was completely normal and wonderful, that we are here to expand and create our own reality. They explained the perspective that if I have more, I am not taking that from someone else. That I can't get poor enough to help the people in the world who don't have enough, or get sick enough to help someone who is ill. There is so much abundance in the world, plenty for everyone, when you don't look at the world from the mindset of lack or scarcity.

Esther and Abraham's teaching on creating your own reality is extensive, but I'll offer a few points and then you can do your own research. They say that you "get out ahead" of life experiences, by deciding to feel good first and not by responding to life. You choose your thoughts and feelings, and get into alignment, which I'll talk about in a bit. Esther and Abraham also say you don't have play by the rules of this reality. Esther jokes about people saying to her, "You can't do this or that, it's not reality." And her response is, "Why would I want your reality, it sounds so dismal. I create my own."

Meditation

I also appreciated the view the Hicks have of meditation. Esther and Abraham say that meditation can quiet the mind, can stop the lower vibration thought, stop resistance which are thoughts that work against you, and make room for inspiration. If you can stay quiet and stay open, you will get an idea or a thought that drops in. If that doesn't work to raise your vibration, or get you in a good mood, take a nap. Your disposition always resets after you sleep because thought stops. I'll talk about vibration later in the section on the Law of Attraction.

During this time I learned as much as I could about meditation through podcasts, books and YouTube. I had such a busy mind and wanted it to be quiet. Besides the different breath related meditations, I found guided meditations that I enjoyed because again, it gave my mind something to focus on. I also did meditations to open the different energy centers of my body. For instance, you can open the third eye chakra for intuition or the heart chakra for love.

Consistent with what Abraham and Esther Hicks talked about, Napoleon Hill backed that up in his book, Think and Grow Rich. He described a way to connect to Infinite Intelligence, as he calls it, through meditation. He says Einstein connected with this source to figure out the parts of a theory that he couldn't access with his "thinking" mind. Connecting to Infinite Intelligence is like connecting with God, or your higher self. I think in many ways it is similar to connecting to your intuition, like Jess Lively shares.

Law of Attraction

Many authors talk about the Law of Attraction, and those who do, refer to it as a universal law. It is like gravity, it acts on you like a force, whether you believe in it or not. The Law of Attraction states that like attracts like, or things of similar vibration attract to each other. So, if you create higher vibration thoughts, like joy or happiness, you will attract similar from life around you. If you create low vibration thoughts, or do so unconsciously, you will attract lower vibration energy in your life.

This is not something I think much about

anymore, but I still think it is happening in the background of our lives. Take for example, first thing in the morning you hit snooze and get a late start on the day. Pouring coffee, you spill some on the floor. Your dog rushes to clean it up and trips one of the kids. Now your child is crying and you husband comes down the stairs and asks what you did, which makes you mad. An unconscious action triggered a string of low-vibe or negative events.

The opposite can also happen. You are up early to meditate and do your gratitude practice and have time to make coffee. Your husband appreciates that so he offers to make you breakfast. Then when the kids come down, he's already cooking and makes them breakfast as well. You can sit and have your coffee before the day gets going. Starting the day off intentionally, keeping the vibration and energy high and positivity attracts more positive outcomes.

To work with the Law of Attraction, I was simply aware of my emotions and actions, and did what I could to influence them to more positivity. I was never someone who was happy all the time, thinking that just wasn't possible for me. I used to blame other people, or my circumstances, until I learned I could choose to think new thoughts for myself and choose my emotional state. I could consciously get into a good feeling mood and that would help to attract other good attitudes, responses and positive interaction from others.

Manifesting in Children

I was starting to share with my kids ideas of manifesting, and law of attraction, and even quantum physics. I would tell them to speak, out loud, for what they want in life, that our words directly affect the outcome of our reality. I also wanted them to understand how changing their energy, or mood causes others to respond to you in a positive way.

My middle child has always been 'lucky', and I have felt that she is more connected to her energy and power than I was. She seems to manifest things on a whim. Take for instance when we were on a road trip to North Carolina and she was saving money to buy an iPod. She found a $50 bill on the ground under a tire when we stopped for lunch.

Or the time she had to run the mile in sixth grade. She complained incessantly to me in the days leading up to it and I reminded her of her power, that a positive spin couldn't hurt. The day she was supposed to run it, it rained all day and was cancelled. The mile got rescheduled and by the time she had to run it, she didn't mind anymore.

My son, the oldest, has done some pretty cool things, too. He joined the lacrosse team his freshman year after having never played before. He started the season off strong, and within the first couple games he scored a couple goals. He still wanted to score more in one game, and just playing around I said, just decide to score three goals, and in a game the next week, he did!

As parents, it's ok to plant ideas of success in your children's heads. In fact, I recommend it. I call it pre-paving and I promise you, the power of suggestion is strong. I'm not saying to tell your child they are the best player on the team when they actually suck, that is not a good idea. I'm just saying sometimes we forget to dream big, help them believe in themselves or even think something is possible. As Abraham and Esther Hicks say, you don't just have to accept this reality, create your own. I think a reality created by our children, free of programming and limited beliefs, would be amazing!

God's Will

It wasn't just that I wanted to see my children get

things they wanted, though that was fun. My world changed when I realized I had more influence in my life. I was raised with this idea that we only prayed for "God's will" and He was in charge, not us. It was such a passive role, almost like driving and taking your hands off the wheel. Not to name any names, but there's a country song that says exactly that!

I thought of my relationship to the Universe, or God more as a co-creation opportunity, we worked together and I spoke up about what I wanted. I also thought about my relationship with other people like this. We could work together to create the experience in life or business we wanted. The programs around what I deserved, around selfishness and even around Heaven and Hell were being changed. I was erasing things that no longer served me, and I hadn't realized were so damaging.

This is very different from how I was raised because in Christianity, there is an authoritative structure that keeps humans in a prostrate position. There is separation between humans and God first because of sin, but then because we are judged in the afterlife. If you take the dogma out, clear those ideas off the table, and look at them with conscious awareness, they don't serve you. In fact, they don't serve anyone except the political and religious leaders of our world today.

Let's get out of this lower vibration and talk about how to get into alignment. That's more fun for everyone!

Getting into Alignment

Alignment is when you get into a good mental and emotional state, or a high vibration, in Law of Attraction terms. To get into alignment, you could read a book, watch a light-hearted tv show, or do a happy dance. I've had fun times dancing and singing in my kitchen to help my kids change their emotional state to a more positive one. If you are starting your day with an alignment practice then you may only want or need to spend a few minutes doing it. However, if you are in the middle of the day, trying to shift from a negative or low vibration, to a higher, positive one, you might need to be more conscious of it.

One of the ways I am more intentionally creating alignment is by journaling or writing positive affirmations, like this famous Emile Coue quote: "Every day, in every way, I am getting better and better." Or saying it out loud with positive, happy emotion, which actually can convince your brain you are happy, thus releasing hormones to cause that feeling. And saying it out loud enacts the laws of Quantum Physics to create your own reality.

If you're having trouble thinking of your own affirmations, I like to turn on a YouTube episode of Esther Hicks (and Abraham) and listen to her do a "Rampage of Appreciation." She just gets me out of my head and feeling good. Like I said, it's motivation from an enlightened source.

Writing to Your Intuition

Writing to your intuition is another practice I learned from Jess Lively. The goal being, quiet the thinking mind and converse directly with your "inner being" or intuition. Often when we are thinking about what to do in a situation, we think to "ourselves" what should I do about this or that? And our thinking mind answers, it might say, "Well you tried this before and tried that before, and now maybe we should just quit." This is just a conversation running circles in your mind, or you could say a conversation of your ego. But when you can quiet that part of your thinking mind, and listen for your intuition, or your heart or gut response, it comes from that deeper place.

Writing to my intuition was one of the first types

of inner work that I did. It is a way to deeply connect to my own guidance system, even though it wasn't always clear. Connect to my soul, instead of my mind and ego.

Digging Deeper

When you are digging for a foundation in the Northern half of the United States, you have to dig deep enough to go below the frost line. That is the line below which the ground freezes – about three feet deep. If you don't pour the footing below that, when the winter comes and the ground freezes, it could buckle your concrete and collapse your building.

The same is true of your inner work. You can scratch the surface of transformation, like I did during my false awakening. You could make great changes in your life, but if they are emulating others, or just running a different program, it won't be authentic for you. I knew I was making progress, pointing in the right direction, but it still seemed superficial and not soul-connected. Values rooted in other people's beliefs won't hold up when the pressure is on. I had to go deeper, I felt it in my whole being.

Transcending Child Consciousness

When my oldest was three and a half years old, we were on our way to the neighborhood park to meet some friends. He was running ahead, excited as always to meet his friends and play for an hour. As we were walking he saw some bigger boys riding bikes. As they passed him, he yelled, "You need helmets guys!"

I laughed and said, encouragingly, "You're right, honey. That isn't safe, is it?" And smiled because it was cute, but also humbling when I saw he was just imitating me. Children learn by watching us, then apply it to their own life, where possible. They don't think for themselves.

And that is what I did with Christianity, I listened to what other people told me and believed it. I didn't think for myself. I was essentially at the level of a child's consciousness, I honestly didn't know how to think for myself, and I didn't know I was allowed to. My awakening helped me to see that I am worthy of making my own decisions. I can think for myself and so can you.

Understanding the concepts of creating my own reality, Law of Attraction and intuition were big shifts for me. I didn't even know these existed, especially the possibility that I could influence the outcome of my life in that way. I had changed my thinking on so many aspects of my life already, things that I didn't even know I could change, and I was just getting started.

6

Ah-ha Moments

The last few months in D.C. were the best months I'd had in quite some time. Largely because of the new ways I was approaching my reality. I was still learning so much, and starting to see how shifting my thinking was affecting my life in tangible, positive ways. On the home front, my husband continued to travel and I wrapped up my part-time job so I could focus on building my new architecture practice.

I don't pretend to know everything about consciousness, but I absolutely loved learning about it. Since I had never read any non-fiction books until now, I had an insatiable desire for knowledge. Besides consciousness related books, I read ones on spirituality, psychology, business, entrepreneurship, and health. I also renewed some of my architectural certifications and memberships as I geared up to start taking on clients. I was expanding my mind in every direction.

The resource list in the back of the book is chronological so you can see the knowledge path I went on. For every book I read, I listened to dozens of podcasts and watched almost that many YouTube videos.

Awareness

The Power of Now, by Eckhart Tolle, is the first spiritual book that I read, and to be perfectly honest at the time I did not really understand the concepts. It teaches a way of being by living in the present moment. I felt like I was stuck in my thoughts, and now I was working on changing my thoughts. The concept Eckhart Tolle was trying to convey is that we can be the objective observer of our thoughts.

We can observe our thoughts, from the perspective of an outsider. He describes it when he says, "The beginning of freedom is the realization that you are not the possessing entity – the thinker.

Knowing this enables you to observe the entity. The moment you start watching the thinker, a higher level of consciousness becomes activated. (Power of Now, 1997, Eckhart Tolle). This concept of awareness, or observing the thinker may take a minute to wrap your head around, because it did for me.

I learn by doing, and as it turns out, vlogging drove this idea home for me. A vlog is like a video blog, where you record everything you do in the day and post it online. I created approximately two hundred videos for my paper crafting business, so I knew how to do video. My favorite videos to create were my annual vlogs where I'd riff about life and business. Taking advice from Gary Vaynerchuk, a serial entrepreneur with a popular vlog, I decided to document my reemergence into my architecture career.

Vlogging

Gary Vaynerchuk says that we should document our process and journey, not create content. I have only ever, created content, basically creating a video specifically for a purpose. This is not the style of video he thought people should be creating in order to build a brand. He suggested we should capture the whole story. That would be so fascinating if we were able to see the journey of Vera Wang when she was first starting off, the good and the bad. Our society wants to see how people became who they are now, context and history, not just the end product. (From his video on YouTube titled: Document, Don't Create).

What happened in this process is I learned about awareness (and self-awareness, as Gary says). One of the first video I recorded, is still on my YouTube channel titled: Vlog Prequel. I was exercising in the workout room at the Avalon apartment, in D.C.. I was holding the camera while recording myself, and saw my reflection in the mirror. And the revelation that occurred to me was, documenting my journey had to be coming from an external perspective. In order to tell the story of my life, I couldn't be the one holding the camera. The objective awareness from the outside was the camera man perspective. This was the awareness to tie in Eckhart Tolle's concept.

This was such a profound truth I had finally understood while vlogging. I am the one thinking the thoughts, and I am also the one observing or watching the thoughts. Many people say they have trouble meditating. This is one of the primary reasons, they are over identified with their thoughts. They don't realize they can create space from them, observe them instead of just taking them as fact.

Make Space in Your Mind

Our awareness acts as a buffer for reactions and can reduce the impact of your response. When you realize you are the awareness of your thoughts, you can be an objective presence in your mind. You witness the thought, listen impartially and do not judge it. It is at this point in which you don't have to let the thoughts run rampant in your mind. By doing this, you are creating space. In this space you can welcome in your own presence, your soul.

I remember when I first started dating my husband and spending time with my in-laws. His mom was always coaching his dad to take a cleansing breath when there was a point he might lose his temper. This usually happened while he was driving or waiting in line for something. Though it was a bit of a joke to them, it was an effective method for creating space in the situation.

When we realize that we are in control of our mind, we regain the power over our conscious thoughts and our reaction to them. Once I understood my thoughts, which are the conscious mind, I could dive into what was even deeper, my unconscious.

I was shifting from praying to God and for God's will to choosing what I wanted to happen, envisioning it and feeling how wonderful it feels to already have it. That is the trick, if you will, of creating you own reality, and using the LOA, is that you feel as though you already have what you want. I was feeling good feeling like opportunities were opening for me and they really did start to open for me.

Manifesting May

In May things were really falling into place, as in I was creating some pretty great things in my reality.

On May 2nd I was heading out to the gym and listening to a podcast from Gary Vaynerchuk. At the end he had a contest that he was promoting where you could win a trip to New York and he would interview you on his podcast! When we moved to D.C., I had the hope of writing a book so that I could be interviewed on podcasts, my 'wish' to the Universe. Though I didn't magically have a book, I got an interview on The Gary Vee Audio Experience, one of the top entrepreneurial podcasts! I won!

I was a pretty big fan of him and loved how he taught me that f*ck isn't such a bad word. My previous programming would not have allowed me to listen to someone with that kind of language. But honestly, I think using the f-bomb can actually be an awakening experience, and a liberating move for many people stuck in a program like I was. Had I not been able to see past that word, I wouldn't have opened myself up to this experience and so much more I learned from him.

I also had this feeling that I wanted to be friends with Gary, not just be a random person he interviews. We were the same age, which I knew because he made a video right before his 40th birthday that went viral. In fact, it's how I found him. The video was called *6 minutes for the Next 60 Years of your Life*. I was also turning 40, and it inspired me so much. I wasn't sure what would come of this, but I was thrilled that I would have the chance to see.

Of course, I hoped that being on Gary's podcast might somehow kick start my career. I can't speak to that right now, but I'll tell you what it did kickstart. My hustle. My interview was scheduled for the end of June, and I worked so hard knowing

Gary Vaynerchuk himself would be holding me accountable. I called it the 'Gary Vee affect'. And I knocked May and June out of the park!

Later in the month, I manifested my first architectural client, a family from Cleveland who was renovating a 1940's home. My husband referred me to the family, as he worked with the wife. We would be gutting the entire home and adding an addition of a basement and bonus room. It was a good-sized project for my first one in nearly ten years.

Lastly, to make this month beyond amazing, I was driving back to D.C. from Ohio on a Sunday evening. I had been infatuated with Frank Lloyd Wright, famous American architect, since getting back into architecture. I realized his masterpiece, Falling Water, was only fifteen minutes off my route. I immediately rerouted and headed to the beautiful home built on a waterfall.

I made it just in time for the last tour of the day, literally as they were starting to walk out of the Visitor's Center. Since it was the last tour of the night, when everyone cleared out, the house was empty, and I was able to linger in each room for just a minute by myself. It was a deeply moving experience to be at Falling Water. I felt like I was reconnecting with my essence somehow. I was starting to believe that we may have soul connections to people or have lived past lives, especially with the example of Abraham Hicks. I thought maybe I was connected somehow to Frank Lloyd Wright, either way, I felt connected.

Synchronicities

I was feeling more connected to everyone and everything, energetically. I was feeling more spiritual, which I think of now as being more connected to my Self. I had learned about synchronicities, and had noticed them happening all of the time. Synchronicities are like signs from God or the Universe, to let you know you're on the right path. In my opinion, they are only as good as your belief in them. If you believe seeing sequential numbers, like 11:11 is good luck, then it is good luck for you.

As I was walking away from Falling Water, I saw a deer running, and I felt like it was the first of many synchronicities that I saw over the next few months. The house is located in what is now called Bear Run Nature Preserve, and a final sign from the Universe as I left the tour in my car, was a black bear cub running across the road right in front of me! It was magical, and I appreciated the added confirmation I received in that moment. All is well.

Almost anywhere since that moment, when I was in nature, especially if I was seeking direction about something, as if praying, I would see at least one deer. They were turning up, to just give me a sense of confidence and remind me I was on the right path.

Accepting What Is

One of the profound practices I have implemented from Eckhart Tolle, is the idea of accepting the "isness" of the situation. Accepting what *is*. If you don't resist it and judge it, you can just accept it and take positive action from that point forward. It may be something good, or something bad, not judging as good or bad is a start because that triggers our emotions to react to it positively or negatively. Accepting the isness of the situation is not judging it. I talk about this later in the book with regard to creating suffering in our minds. Instead, take aligned action if necessary, or let it go.

In the midst of all these things I saw unfolding, I had something that didn't go as planned. My podcast with Gary Vaynerchuk, got cancelled. The week I was supposed to go to New York, I got an email from his team and they said he was unable to keep our meeting. I understood, he was a busy guy, and it was the same week as his new show from Apple went live. I couldn't imagine the pressures on him this week. He was starring in *Planet of the Apps,* seriously, he was on the Today Show that week!

Vayner Media had already paid for train tickets, so my son and I ended up making the trip anyway. We had never taken the train from D.C. to New York City before and it sounded like a fun weekend away. Gary's team was nice enough to invite us to stop by Vayner Media offices and take a tour while we were there. I passed on the chance to take pictures inside Gary's office. I felt like that wouldn't be right, I would take pictures next time, when I was invited back for the interview.

Meeting Gary Vaynerchuk

We waited at Vayner Media until Gary was finished with his meeting, and my son and I rode down the elevator with him and several other people. I was able to say hello and introduce myself before he left for his next meeting. He was such a genuine, kind human being, and I appreciate just being able to meet him in real life. He assured me that we would reschedule for the fall.

I didn't leave completely empty handed. My son pointed out that I got a kiss on the check from Gary Vaynerchuk, and with that, we took our selfie's and said goodbye. We made our way back to Washington, D.C. to pack and move back to Ohio. The interview never got scheduled, it just wasn't meant to be at that moment in time.

I gave it some thought at first, wondering if I did something wrong or if they changed their mind because I am this *nobody* mom from Ohio. There were a lot of things that went through my mind with this idea of rejection. And then I reframed it, and really accepted it for the lesson I could learn from this. It wasn't rejection, it all happened how it was supposed to happen. Had I had the interview at that time, when I had been vlogging for two months but had no experience behind me in business, no book to speak of, barely an opinion to discuss with him, it would have failed miserably. It wasn't meant to be.

Now, two plus years later, after so much growth and awareness, I could have a more meaningful conversation with him. Then I was a child, just doing what he told me to do, and doing what he does, I was still not thinking for myself. That was at the beginning of my awakening and I am so thankful for his influence with vlogging and self-awareness, because I was able to capture so much of my transformation in those first fifty VLOG episodes I did. And, I am still open to scheduling that interview, just for the record. It would just be a much more interesting discussion now than it would have been in June of 2017. While I'm on the topic, feel free to Google him, but I'd like to take some liberties of my own and use him as an example.

Formulas and Programs

I think Gary Vaynerchuk is a great example of someone who is much closer to having the ideal "formula" than most people. He seems to be free of much of the lower states of consciousness and programming that many Americans are entrenched in. It's like he has grown up with all the positive programming and none of the religious or even the American Dream programming, as I discussed in the first chapter, that people born here have.

He came to the United States from Russia when he was very young, and so I would speculate that they were not yet entrenched in American culture. Instead of taking it for granted, they passed on to their children a perspective of appreciation instead of entitlement.

From what I have seen in the past few years of Gary Vaynerchuk's growth and evolution, he is someone who defaults to his own intuition, whereas the rest of us are looking for the answer outside of ourselves. He jokes about being lucky, to be born in Russia, to have the parents he did, to have the mindset instilled in him with the right balance of gratitude and hard work. He is right, he was lucky. The formula that created him gave him the capacity to create his own program, and to experience freedom in a truth of his own.

So what about the rest of us? The formula that created each and every one of us is different, and all of the factors that I mentioned play into it, including any trauma you've experienced, the time and location of your birth. Maybe you were lucky, or maybe not, you can still have all the same choices for your life. You may just have to choose them consciously. Luck is unconscious, choice is conscious. There may be nothing you feel you can do about luck, which is why you can choose.

7

Individuation
July - December 2017

Shortly after my trip to meet Gary Vaynerchuk, we had to move ourselves back to Ohio. Of course, it was another ninety-five-degree day in July, apparently we had not learned our lesson the first time. My husband was planning to move into a hotel for the remaining six-months, not a bad gig, but he helped us move and then returned to D.C.. I would be a single mom with the kids and dog in Canton.

In coming back to Ohio, nearly everything was

the same except me, I was different. I was proud of my growth and change, but I was scared too. This change in me from traditional Midwest views of God and religion, were gone and I was on a new path that didn't involve anyone or anything I had known a year ago. My inclination was to lay low. I felt vulnerable because I was still forming my identity. I was like a butterfly still inside the chrysalis, finishing its transformation and gaining its strength to emerge.

I saw meditation as an important tool for connecting to my intuition and gaining the space I wanted in my thinking mind. I just happened to know a teacher of Transcendental Meditation (TM).

Transcendental Meditation

It so happened that the TM instructor was also the developer for a community of meditators in Canton. Not just a community group, an actual physical neighborhood. He was selling lots for single-family homes, in a community that would be *green* and sustainably focused, which was exciting to think about being part of.

I wanted to learn an official meditation technique. I recognize now, in hindsight, that part of this desire was my type-A personality needing to know how to do it "right." Now I know there is no right or wrong way to meditate. Regardless, I took the TM course over a few days and learned a lot about brain wave activity and the mind. I was assigned a mantra, which is a phrase that you say over and over in your mind during meditation to focus.

I practiced Transcendental Meditation for several months, but as much as I believe that technique is good for reducing stress and everything it is advertised to be, it was too rigid for me. I wanted to connect to my soul, to my highest self, and even my genius as many people including Einstein believed possible. Transcendental Meditation, I feel, keeps people in their brains but I wanted to go beyond the mind.

I appreciate having TM in my toolkit of practices, but my meditation now looks very different. I often focus on an intention, or just open my mind to time with no thoughts. My meditation is sometimes intense, quiet focus. Other times I just sit and take a few deep breaths. It's all good for you and it can be five minutes or fifty-five minutes long. I share some meditation ideas on my podcast, The Amy Kunkle Audio Hour, which you can find on any podcast app or just the old-fashioned internet.

I like to meditate every day, even if it's just for a few minutes. I find if I miss meditating I can more easily fall back into unconscious behavior and programs from my past. During the school year I meditate after the kids are out of the house, during the summer I sit outside and ground myself to the earth. Sunday mornings became a wonderful time for me to spend in meditation, since I wouldn't be going back to church.

Quietly Quitting Church

I had a plan in my mind that I would meet with our pastor, a friend of mine and share my amazing awakening. It really felt like a liberation I wanted to share. I quickly came to my senses. I figured, when you leave a church, they don't typically high-five you on the way out. Switching churches is one thing, perhaps going to where you like the music better or get along better with the teachers, is fairly common amongst the non-denominational Christian churches.

Leaving because you don't believe the message that is preached from the pulpit, that is different. I didn't believe that humans were inherently sinners, or that Jesus died on the cross to save us from the judgement of hell. No, I couldn't believe in it anymore. I believe we continue to evolve and transition into non-physical, aka our spirit goes back into spirit and our bodies decay.

If you are wondering if I ever considered staying at the church, attending and just not fully believing, the answer is no. I wasn't going to stay for the fellowship or the children programs. I wasn't mad at anyone or angry, but I also couldn't support this system that was keeping people separate from God. I thought becoming a Christian was a more direct connection to God than Catholicism was. But now I see Christianity as yet another barrier to our own divine nature.

Nature is My Church

When I was starting my architecture practice, I poured over a book by Frank Lloyd Wright, called The Testament. It is a combination of memoir and his benediction to the world which he wrote near the end of this life. One of the things that caught my attention is that he was raised in the Midwest and had a father who was a minister. He talks about his religious beliefs in the book and says he attends no church. He said, "I put a capitol 'N' on Nature and that is my church."

I'm with him. I connect to the stillness of Nature and feel God. I don't attend a church anymore, I seek my own intuition and soul guidance. I believe Jesus was an enlightened human being, not the son of God.

I have a wooden sign in my house that says: "Be Still and Know that I am God." At first I was going to just pitch it. No reason to have Bible verses around the house, right? But then I saw the deeper meaning, and kept it because I truly believe that in the stillness, we can know that we connect to the aspect of God in ourselves. I am not saying I am God. I believe God is an energetic and creative force, not a person. I like the analogy that the Universe, or God is the ocean, and we are a wave.

Opening up to Friends

I couldn't stay hidden away forever, so I decided to try explaining my awakening to some of my close friends. I was new at explaining it and I'm sure it came out all wrong. I didn't have my "new beliefs" dialed in, but I knew I had to have answers for the people in my life, including acquaintances. I felt that I was justifying myself a bit, but it just made functioning in the world easier if I knew what I was going to tell people.

I ran into one woman from church in the lobby of a restaurant. She assumed that I had changed churches. I said no, I quit going because I don't believe any of it anymore. She was taken aback, and said that it was too bad. I decided I needed a better response, should that ever happen again.

For my friends, I told them that I just don't think that God would have wanted us to create these religions in His name. I also said I don't know if God is a He or a She but probably just energy, and I don't think heaven or hell is real. I also believe in past lives and possibly reincarnation. It was a lot, but if they had more questions I was also ok saying, I don't know.

It is obviously very different from what I believed as a Christian. I knew I would get mixed responses, and I was just thankful they came from my friends. My husband was a completely different situation. He was home about one weekend every month or so at this point and we didn't breach the subject of what I actually believed very often. When we did it was intense.

Being Interrogated

If he wasn't actually trained by the government to interrogate people, this would be funny. As it stands, it was no joke. I felt like talking to him about what I believed was an interrogation. We would always be standing at the kitchen island, face to face when he was rattling off questions.

I remember saying, almost as if a confession, "I don't think I believe in God anymore, and I don't believe we are sinners."

To which he responded, "If we are not sinners, why is there still evil in the world?"

At that point in time, I really didn't know what I believed about that. "Yeah, I don't know that answer." I replied.

"If you don't believe in God, do you still believe in Jesus?" He said next.

Thinking for a minute, "Yes, I do believe Jesus lived but not sure about the son of God part."

Ultimately, he would get the best of me and I would just end up frustrated because I couldn't answer his questions. These conversations were usually pretty short, for obvious reasons. I told myself it was ok, because I was still working through it all and he was only in town for one weekend a month. But it shouldn't have been ok, I should have tried to bring him in sooner. Instead, I was doing all of this internal work and he wasn't. I think he saw it as personal development. I saw it as evolution. I was evolving and he wasn't.

8

Energy Distribution

Realizing that human beings are made of energy was a huge trigger in my awakening, and I want to cover why that was, now before I get too far. There were so many insightful teachings from scientist and author, Dr. Joe Dispenza, I was really creating a whole new me from the inside out.

Dr. Joe Dispenza is a researcher who studies neuroscience, epigenetics, quantum physics and spontaneous remissions. To put it plainly, he studies energy. As much as that sounds very science-based, he opens his book, *Becoming*

Supernatural, with an explanation of having a mystical, transcendental moment in his life, something science will probably never be able to explain. I'll let you do your own research, but I hope this discussion helps to peak your curiosity.

I have already talked about creating your own reality, in chapter five, Fading to Black. Now I will share how all of this really sunk in to my analytical, left brain. Deep down, I have always thought in terms of left and right brain functions. Now, ironically, science has proven that both of our brain hemispheres work together. Which I love because that shows our brain is actually co-creating. That is what you call evolution, baby.

Thinking your Thoughts

Ultimately, this is about our thoughts. You are the one creating and thinking them, so start doing it more consciously. Dr. Joe Dispenza has said recently that thoughts create an electrical charge and feeling create a magnetic charge. Let that sink in a minute if you need to. It is all energy and we are the creator and the awareness, as Eckhart Tolle says.

Most of the time we think we are just stuck with our personality, not realizing we created it by one small thought after another. Dr. Joe says, if you track your personality back, it began by having a thought that you let repeat long enough that it became a mood. That mood stayed long enough to create a temperament, and that temperament stayed long enough to become your personality. This is why some people seem like a "glass is half empty" type of person, they got stuck in a pattern of thought and that became their personality and their *now* reality.

The kids and I had moved back to Ohio and I was a single mom at this point, ready for some time to let all of this sink in. You have to let things sink in sometimes. Like when you water a plant way too fast, you have to pause for a minute to let the water absorb.

Working Mom

Being a mom and working takes a good amount of energy, especially when your partner isn't around to help. Upon moving back to Canton, I had arranged to open my own office with a local civil engineer. He was leasing the space, and I signed on for a year as my business was so new I didn't want to over commit myself. He had an established business and was looking for an architect to team with, and needed to move his office out of his home as well. Turns out working from home can be a juggling act for anyone.

I moved into my office space in the fall after school kicked off for the year. The office was on the top floor of an eight story building, and had a great view of the sunset for times I worked late. Which wasn't often, but was an added bonus when I did. I had one client at this time who's project was under construction, by now, so my days were filled mostly with research and marketing.

I spent some time helping my Transcendental Meditation instructor, also developer, create guidelines for his "green" neighborhood. I was also honing my niche as a Conscious Architect, and defining what that meant to me. I continued vlogging and posting online, starting to share more about my new conscious perspective, especially as it tied into the design of our built environment.

As a mom, I don't have an excuse to travel much, so when I did my paper crafting business I would attend conferences every year, and honestly, I really just love in person events. I hope to have my own events someday, wink wink to the Universe. It had been a couple years since I'd been to a conference, and I had never been to a personal development conference before, so I was due. I was a "conscious achiever" as Lewis Howes calls it, and this conference was made for me. It was the Summit of Greatness, annual conference in Columbus, Ohio, run by podcaster and influencer, Lewis Howes. It was a great conference, but I want to talk about something I spent a good amount of energy on this particular fall. Healing my allergies.

Healing Allergies

I have been allergic to tree nuts since I was little, probably ten years old. That includes pecans, almonds, pistachios, walnuts, but NOT peanuts, they are legumes. If I had a dollar for every time I said that... My doctor prescribed an epi-pen just in case my throat would swell closed, although it's never been that serious. Walnuts never seemed to follow suit though, so if you want a good laugh, you can see what happens when I had walnuts for lunch during the Summit of Greatness conference. It's Vlog 48 and is listed in the resource section. I was working on healing my tree nut allergy, which probably seems strange, but hear me out.

Jess Lively talked about healing her eyesight on an episode of her podcast, The Lively Show Episode 242. She read Dr. Jacob Liberman's book *Take off Your Glasses and See*, and had him on the podcast. He was able to heal his eyesight by healing his shadow, aka doing the inner work and focusing energy on it. I decided it couldn't hurt to try, I have always wanted to try pecan pie.

I started with my thoughts, and by telling myself and people around me that our bodies regenerate every seven years. I was using this fact in changing my thinking about allergies, and reprogramming my brain. I also started to explain to people that we can create our own reality, and I learned that my allergies could be under my control. I didn't connect my allergy to tree nuts to any unconscious shadow or trauma, but I will discuss that later in the book. At this point, I was working strictly with changing my thoughts about the allergy.

I started experimenting with almonds. They didn't seem to bother me as much, maybe they were more dried out during their processing. I ate a chocolate covered almond and had no reaction, woo-hoo! I had a pine nut, garlic and olive oil pizza topping, yay! The highlight, so far, in my allergy-free journey, was sharing a piece of pecan pie with my sister, when I was in town for my mom's wedding. I had no reaction whatsoever.

Energy And Where It Goes

It was shortly after this experimenting with tree

nuts that I realized I was spending a lot of my energy focusing on getting rid of my tree nut allergy. Which was fine, but with the walnut mishap, it obviously wasn't cured. I had a lot of other things going on in my life that I wanted to see transformation in. Other areas of my health, for instance, and my career. I felt like I had a limited amount of energy, and wanted to be conscious of how I was "using" it.

As humans, we can expend energy in physical ways. Exercising, eating, breathing, and living in the world uses energy. But we also use energy in non-physical, mental ways. Thinking, worrying and even consciously creating our own reality uses energy. What I really wanted was a balance in this fluctuation of energy. I still seemed very mental and mind focused, I was in my head and not connecting to my soul.

This was when I discovered Julie Piatt, who is a modern day mystic and mother, known as SriMati. I found her through a podcast I listened to by her husband, Rich Roll. Julie has a podcast called *For The Life Of Me*, where she offers a spiritual perspective on our human experience. I loved how spiritual she was, and connected to her divine self, as she called it. She uses words like sacred moment, divine emanation of God, and shared healing techniques on her podcast. The techniques were focused on energetic healing. They ranged from meditations on love and expansion to sexual healing and creativity. I used many of her healings to bridge this gap I felt of being in my head and learning this practice of connecting more deeply with my soul and my heart.

Healing seemed to be a large part of this journey of awakening. It wasn't just about awareness and making space, but healing the past and healing the unconscious parts of yourself. Some of this can be achieved through meditations like Julie offers, but there are many healing modalities available today, some of which I tried and talk about in the next chapter.

Moon Cycles

I love when science intersects with spirituality, because they validate each other. The moon cycles affect our energy, and before I realized that, I just thought some weeks I was productive and other weeks I wasn't. Not realizing it had so much to do with the earth and moon cycles and not my fault.

Through Jess Lively, I found Dr. Ezzie Spencer, author of *Lunar Abundance*: *Cultivating Joy, Peace and*

Purpose Using the Phases of the Moon. I have learned so much from her about the cycles of the moon and how to set intentions, when to take action, and when to release something that is not aligning. It is so amazing when you work with your energy, instead of against it.

When I am organized enough to plan out my month in advance, and set goals, I do them around the fluctuation of energy I know I will have. I am just setting myself up for success, knowing when during the month I will want to push and when I'll want to chill. I like having some practices focused around the moon cycles. I also have practices around the change of seasons, which applies here as well.

The practices usually include yoga or meditation, setting intentions and writing goals, or even something fun, and I want to say completely impractical here, like setting my crystals out in the moonlight. Did you know you can charge your crystals with the energy of the moon? Have you heard of sun gazing? Oh the fun you can have when you are just open to trying new things! I won't talk about sun gazing, so you'll just have to use your thumbs and Google that.

Practices can be good, when they are done

consciously. If you do a practice or habit so long that it lacks meaning, and ends up being done unconsciously, then I would release it. Quit, let it go, change and find something that aligns better. Letting go of old habits can be just as important as starting new ones.

Practices and Habits

My brother, Steve, is a great example of someone who looks consciously at his habits, identifies what is and is not serving him, and adjusts accordingly. Last year he decided to quit drinking for the entire year. It was a great way to reset his programming around drinking, and after the year was over, he added some alcohol back into his life, consciously. Meaning, he did it with intention and awareness around the issue.

However, sometimes our commitment, even to good things, can become more about our ego and accomplishing something. Steve also started a morning routine about the same time. He is an entrepreneur and business owner and was looking for a way to up level his life.

He would get up at 5:00 AM, exercise and get to his office before his employees did. He would also end his day reading and learning for an hour.

Both great practices to be doing.

The problem came when he had a new baby in the house. Lack of sleep and a busy work schedule challenged his morning workout time and his evening learning hour. But he pushed through. He kept up this rigorous schedule and seemed to be continually sick, and mentally, and physically exhausted. I suggested his body was trying to tell him something, and I encouraged him to let some of these practices go for now.

Keeping any practice while you ignore what your body or soul is telling you, isn't worth it. You can let it go. The activities we invest our time into all use up our energy, so be conscious of what you choose to add into or take out of your life.

Crystals, Grounding and Sex Energy

I don't talk about these things anywhere else in the book, but wanted to share since I am on the topic of energy. My disclaimer to this section is that these energy hacks, not fully developed practices. I am no expert, I just appreciate the value they bring to my life. You're thinking, sex is in the title so she must be talking about that. Sure, but no, I am just talking about doing things in life that are fun, and spark joy, as Marie Kondo says in *The Life-Changing*

Magic of Tidying Up: The Japanese Art of Decluttering and Organizing.

I think crystals are beautiful and I have learned that their structural make up and energy can balance my own. With that said, I buy ones that I think are pretty and feel good when I hold or touch them. You can learn a ton of information about different crystals and how and why they help you, but I will most likely never be the expert on them. When I build a home for myself, I would love to include crystals in parts of my home, and I would consult an expert on crystals when that time comes.

Grounding is another concept I only know enough to share a snippet here. My understanding of it has to do with the earth's energetic force as it relates to my own. When your body gets in contact with the earth, be that grass or concrete, anything that does not prevent the flow of energy, like rubber soles on our shoes. You can balance your energy. The earth has a magnetic pull, and our bodies have energy centers, and spending time in contact with the earth balances your body. If it sounds fun to you, give it a try, it can't hurt.

The last energy hack I'd like to share is how to create energy yourself. You can do this with a partner, wink wink, or by yourself. The idea is that our sacral chakra, located in the area of your sex organs, has the ability to create magnetism and energy that you can use to go stimulate your mind, and what is commonly responsible for psychic or intuitive connection, the pineal gland. Napoleon Hill talks about it as the sex drive, not necessarily the act itself, but the desire behind sex. In his book, *Think and Grow Rich,* he calls this energy creation *Sex Transmutation,* because we are transmuting this feeling of desire (or orgasm possibly) into energy we can use. Now that you're fully awake, have fun with that, and we shall continue on.

Amy M. Kunkle

9

Healing the Unconscious

This was a turning point in my transformation, and maybe for you as well. Many people miss the healing part. In my false awakening, I missed the healing part. This is the adjustment we all need to become whole and helps us to change. Healing can break us free from the program we have been running, help us create the life we want that is in alignment with our highest self. And as a bonus we don't screw up the generation after us, and we collectively heal our planet.

The people that need healing are not just the

fundamental Christians. Please let that sink in. It's easy to point fingers and say <u>that</u> program is screwed up, but maybe you didn't grow up with that. You still have a program you are running. Everyone has something in their own operating system, or unconscious, that is directing their life, and would benefit from healing.

It's possible you don't have any unconscious program, but more likely you are in denial. That is like saying you are completely aware and conscious of everything going on in your mind. Let's go with this hypothetical though, just for the sake of exploring it. If you were raised with the exact right formula to create the person you are, free of emotional baggage or psychological damage, you lucked out. I mentioned Gary Vaynerchuk is lucky, and he even says that about himself. However, there are still fears and unknowns in everyone's life that can control their thoughts, and in turn, their reality.

It is also possible that you may have had someone in your lineage who has already healed it for you. In my opinion, this is the type of thing that is quite difficult to prove. However, in the Bible when it talks about the sins of your fathers being passed down generations, I believe that is what I talking about. If you heal your unconscious shadow, you are correcting the course for future generations. I will flesh out this idea in the coming chapter, so let's get into it.

Shadow and Pain-body

Until 2019, when publishing this book, my knowledge of Carl Jung was miniscule. I used the term "shadow" because other spiritual people used it, but it came from him. At this time in my transformation, I was familiar with the term pain-body, which is from Eckhart Tolle so I will explain the difference because I think they are both important and I will discuss both.

When you want to do the work to become whole, you need to acknowledge unconscious beliefs or patterns that are not healthy and resolve them, or integrate them. That is easier said than done because they are unconscious, as in below your consciousness. And, there are lots of people that don't want to do this work because it can be difficult, and have a possible stigma associated with it, much like going to see a therapist. You only go to a therapist if you acknowledge there is something you need help on, and lots of people aren't willing to admit that. They prefer to stay unconscious, trying to scoop water out of their sinking ship. Or they think it's just God's will that this or that happened, when it was unconscious aspects of themselves rearing its ugly head.

Shadow is a broad term that refers to our dark, negative character traits, or programs, that we are not consciously aware of. Carl Jung coined the term and describes shadow as those aspects of the identity that we chose to reject and repress. He says that the shadow is inferred from the contents of the personal unconscious. (*Aion*, Carl Jung) There are also aspects of the collective unconscious that impact us, and those are inferred from cultural and religious influence, or programs as I have previously discussed.

Eckhart Tolle calls this the pain-body. It is the remnants of pain left behind by every strong negative emotion that is not fully faced, accepted, and then let go of and joins together to form an energy field that lives in the very cells of your body. (*A New Earth*, Eckhart Tolle) He also says this pain is not only in the individual, there is a collective pain-body that all humans share. The collective pain-body is created from the pain and suffering of humanity as a whole.

I use both terms, and will share examples of unconscious programming that falls into both categories of shadow and pain-body. You are lucky if you can approach your unconscious beliefs from a proactive perspective. Usually they take you by surprise like a break-down or mid-life crisis. I began looking at areas of my life that I felt blocked in, where I have not seen success, or have experienced failure, struggle or discontentment.

Pain-body Creation

When I was a newborn, I rejected my mother's breastmilk, the doctors didn't really know why. I also developed really bad eczema and asthma as an infant and child. Once I found out some things that happened around the time of my birth, I wondered if some of my relationship problems stemmed from something my mother was actually experiencing while she was pregnant with me. I should say now, I do not blame my mother at all, just as I do not blame myself in my own children's' pain body creation. It is unconsciously transmitted, just like heat flows through metal, positive and negative energy is passed through from mom to baby.

My parents were both very young, my mom was seventeen when she had my sister, and I was born less than a year later, three hundred and sixty days to be exact, we are the same age for five days. In between having my sister and me, my parents decided to pack up everything into a van and head west. I like to think I was born in the "spirit of adventure" in Great Falls, Montana.

I can only imagine this was a stressful time in my parents lives, being so young with two babies. They were trying to make it on their own, thousands of miles from home. On top of that, my parents were having their own marriage issues. I don't want to get into that story, since it's not my story to tell. I will say, there was a time when my mom was pregnant and after I was born, that she experienced many things I can only imagine as heart breaking and incredibly difficult. I am confident that as a baby in her stomach, not only was I getting nutrients from her, I was also getting energy and emotion.

I don't know for sure this created relationship issues for me, caused feelings of low self-esteem or self-worth, but a myriad of shadow traits could have developed. My intuition knew that it was a possibility, and I was willing to bring it into the light and counter act it by adding in positive thoughts. Even if this wasn't the stem of my self-worth or didn't affect my ability to give or receive love, it would help reinforce the positive vibration that I wanted anyway.

Using Affirmations

One of the first things I tried when I became aware of my potential pain-body related to relationships and self-worth was using affirmations. Affirmations are phrases or sayings that inspire positivity. You can find many examples online, as well as meditations that help you to really connect the affirmation to your heart. It can be a simple practice of writing or saying phrases out loud. It may seem trite, but saying I love and appreciate you in the mirror, or quietly to myself was a valuable integration technique. And it's free!

I spent about two weeks with an affirmation I found in the book, *The Master Key System*, by Charles F. Haanel. The affirmation is, "I am whole, perfect, strong, powerful, loving, harmonious and happy." Another affirmation I really like from Abraham and Esther Hicks is, "Things are always working out for me," which really applies to any situation in life! I would write it on the white board in my home office or put it on a note card on my bathroom mirror or visor in my car. Affirmations are best when said aloud so don't forget to say them with positive emotion, to connect them to your heart, as I discussed in the chapter on energy.

Adults aren't the only ones who can have pain-body or shadow show up, just as mine did when I had eczema. The negative aspects can manifest in many different ways, at any age, it may look like moodiness, anxiety, or even disease. I was experimenting with several different types of healing, so let's move on.

Hypnotherapy

When I heard about hypnotherapy, it made perfect sense that we could dive into our unconscious or subconscious as it is also called, through hypnosis. In fact, many of the meditations online or included in online workshops to reprogram your unconscious use hypnosis. The goal is for you to uncover the origin of your shadow or pain-body since its hiding in there. Once you get to the place in your hypnotherapy session where you have uncovered the incident or root cause, the practitioner will add in the program you want, the healthy, more constructive belief.

I am game to try nearly anything, so, I found a woman who did traditional hypnotherapy at a holistic center in town. The practitioner was running a special on three sessions of hypnotherapy or reiki. Being new to these practices, I opted to try them both. My hypnotherapy session was around the idea of abundance and the opposite, a lack of money. I was working through frustrations I had in starting my business and not achieving the financial goals I had.

During the hypnotherapy session, the room was lit by candles and had soft music playing, much like a massage. In the session, she walked me down a staircase, in my mind and in hushed tones we discussed a scene from my early childhood. I was with my mother, and I was young, maybe 3 or 4. My mom was upset because we were losing money and had to move again. This memory could have caused me to feel a scarcity mentality as an adult, or a fear around losing something because of money.

The practitioner then asked me to change the story around the situation. To reassure the child that it will be ok, that there is plenty of money, that money comes in unexpected ways. I learned during this process, that positive affirmations work on a conscious and unconscious level.

If you are interested in exploring hypnotherapy, be open minded and try different practitioners. Everyone connects differently to other people and you may feel more aligned with one person over another.

Reiki Energy Healing

The other healing modality I had never heard of before was Reiki. Reiki is a Japanese healing technique that uses Universal life-force energy, also called Chi which I learned from doing Acupuncture years ago. The practitioner channels energy from the universe through the energy centers on the body, called the chakras. We have six energy centers, I will list them here for reference. At the base of our spine is our root chakra, then going up is our sacral chakra, our solar plexus chakra, our heart chakra, our throat chakra, then between our eyes is our third eye chakra and at the top of our head is our crown chakra.

It made total sense to me, if our bodies are made of energy that we should have Reiki treatments to balance and clear any blocked energy in our bodies. Blocked energy can cause everything from indigestion to cancer (Dr. Joe Dispenza, *Becoming Supernatural*). Blocked energy can also be caused by shadow or the pain-body, so you see the correlation here. Each chakra corresponds to an area of our health or life that it tends to influence. For instance, the root chakra is our connection to Mother Earth and influences our passion, creativity, safety and security. If your root chakra is out of balance it may be due to the loss of a job or relationship woes.

In my session, the room was set up like a massage, with soft music and candles. The session was mostly hands-off, where the practitioner hoovered her hands over my body. When she would hover over some of my energy centers, I felt intense warmth, not to the point of being uncomfortable, but I could feel an influx of energy.

I enjoyed my Reiki sessions, and at this stage in my transformation, it was exactly what I needed. I loved how I could feel the energy, it was magical and I brought that feeling with me home. I couldn't wait to share this experience with my kids. Reiki is something that I have kept in my "took kit" of healing modalities.

Bedtime Routines

It had been our habit since the kids were little to tuck them into bed at night, with a prayer and hug and kiss. Sometimes I would massage them, especially my youngest, since she was always sore from gymnastics. But one night, I decided to offer Reiki to them. I didn't get super woo woo, I just told them about my experience and asked them if they wanted me to try it on them.

So, while tucking the kids in, I just hover my

hands over their six energy centers, for just a few seconds each. Depending on how much time I can or am able to spend, it may be three seconds on each, or usually it's more like ten seconds on each. I usually just wait for it to heat up and then move on. I also repeated a technique the Reiki practitioner did, even though I didn't quite understand it at the time. I used my hand to brush along their arm, from shoulder to hand in a quick motion. It was as if I was dusting them off. My reiki practitioner said it was a way to get rid of "heavy" or blocked energy.

I would silently offer blessings over them, and appreciation and love while I would warm up their chakras. Actually, my new reiki practitioner said its them providing the energy and warmth, the hands hovering, or lightly laying on them are just conducting it, if that makes sense. Either way, I just like spending more time with my children, helping them to feel my love and connecting to them. In my experience, kids need more time with us, and more connection, so it's a win for both of us. It was also a way I was able to share some of the new me, which I had not been doing. I was slowly figuring things out, and sharing some here and there.

Praying Changed For Me

Now that I didn't believe in God in the same way, I was at a loss for what to do at bedtime besides just the reiki. For a little while I'd ask the kids to pray, and I didn't want to make it awkward, so sometimes I would just pray in a really generic way, if that is possible. Which is possible, if you're wondering.

I figured prayers could be directed to the Universe, they didn't only need to be offered to the long-haired, robed man we have been taught to pray to. I had watched several of Gabby Bernstein's YouTube videos, author of *The Universe has Your Back,* and it seemed like in her meditations she was praying. I was pretty sure she wasn't praying to the previously mentioned God, but the Universe, as her book title suggests. So, I decided to give it a try.

I was thankful the kids were light-hearted about my awakening, because what happened next was downright hilarious. I told my youngest daughter that I wanted to try and pray in my way, and she was game. I started a bit generally, thinking of it as a gratitude exercise. "Thank you, Divine Creator, for breath and life." I don't remember the exact words I said that, but I do remember the ending, and so does she. I closed the prayer as reverently as

I could and said, "The End."

We laughed, and I hugged and kissed her goodnight. I honestly didn't know what else I would end my prayer with... Amen just didn't seem right. It made me think of the scene in Anne of Green Gables where Anne is praying for the first time and she closes her prayer with, "Sincerely Yours, Anne." Thankfully we are all learning through this experience and aren't taking ourselves too seriously.

Healing in Children

My youngest child projectile vomited for nearly the first year of her life. Not every feeding, but about once per day. She also had breathing issues, and allergies that developed as a young child. She also had what seemed like panic attacks even though her pediatrician said she was too young for them. I could see a pain-body in action if I had ever seen one. I wasn't going to let this go, I needed to help her heal now.

She was born at a very stressful time in our lives. She was due the week that my husband was scheduled to leave for six months. We all knew if she didn't come on time that he wouldn't be there for the birth. But, thankfully, she did come into the world, just in time for her daddy to meet her and then two days later he flew out. We were living in Sacramento and not too long after she was born, my in-laws drove with us to Indianapolis where we would live until we got our next assignment. We moved there temporarily to live near my in-laws since they were semi-retired and would be able to help with my three children, all under the age of five.

I was working through my own frustration with being in that situation, and there were a million things I would have done differently. I am sure there were things that didn't matter that much in the whole scheme of things that I could have let go, or changed. There were things that I could have had more awareness around, and yet, I did the best I could with the consciousness I had. Our small apartment was full of fighting with the kids as I was struggling to keep it together.

Back to my youngest, I believe many of the physical symptoms she was experiencing were the direct result of the stress around her birth, and those first six months. As her mother, I admit that I unconsciously created it for her, meaning I had little to no clue at the lasting results of the intense stress of this situation. Only in retrospect am I able to see a physical manifestation of this unconscious pain-body.

I don't know if every negative experience children have is tied to physical symptoms like this, but some of them are and it is worth considering. Let me remind you, as I remind myself, we do the best we can with the tools we have. I didn't know that I could look at the situation differently, but I do now, and so can you.

Connecting to Your Breath

If I had gone to a holistic practitioner, I think I would have been introduced to options other than a nebulizer with a steroid for her breathing issues, and an epi-pen for her allergies. Those issues seemed to get resolved, and at that point, I didn't know any better than to believe what the doctor told me and treat the symptoms. But after my experience with my own anxiety, and my awakening, I knew was going to trust my own intuition on the panic attacks. I decided to help her apply what worked for me.

If she started to inch towards an outburst or tantrum, I would get her to breathe with me, and I would be as present as possible. Meaning, I would get right in her space, hold her if she would let me, look into her eyes and spend focused time with her. I was helping her to connect to her breath and in turn, her Self, and focusing on the present moment.

Sometimes as parents we can lose our temper and get upset because our child is crying and won't stop, especially as they get old enough to understand what we are saying. She may not know how to deal with the pressure building up inside her. We just need to let it release without judgment or punishment. By recognizing she was upset, letting her be upset and just being with her would calm her down. Kids don't always know how to deal with life stressors and connect to their emotions, so going back to the breath and focusing on the present can help.

Compassion for Yourself

I know many people have endured three children under the age of five, and even alone without a spouse, so this situation may not seem that bad. I just know how my daughter's pain-body was created, and possibly that you may have unconsciously contributed to your own children's pain-body. It happens unconsciously amidst turmoil and stress, so all you can do is be aware of it, and if it's in the past, help your children to heal. If you are living this right now, maybe something I share can help you get through.

When parents joke about how they scarred their children by something they did, it is no joke. I fully believe that all of my children will need to heal from this trauma they experienced. I hope as a mother I can have the humility to be open with my children about this, and of course, they can read it in here now. I also hope you can open up to your children about times when you have experienced something like this. You may not have known this was possible, and neither did I, so have compassion for yourself.

As a bit of encouragement, Eckhart Tolle says that people with a heavy pain-body usually have a better chance to awaken spiritually than someone who has a light one. (*A New Earth*, Eckhart Tolle) I think the same thing is true of people who have gone through major trauma or heartache, they are more likely to awaken spiritually. Awakening spiritually is a good thing. This is the journey I am on, and maybe the one you are on as well.

10

It's Getting Real
January – June 2018

As Carl Jung says, you can't integrate on a mountain top. I needed to emerge from my own cave and start living life as it would be. I was doing this work, the healing and integrating, but my husband, my partner had not seen or understood this process. I was unveiling it to him and the world, as it were.

Since my husband was not living with us, I felt like he wasn't part of it at all. Not to mention, he was not on this journey of spiritual awakening either. He didn't have an awakening and mine did not rub off on him. He was a committed Christian and nothing I was going through would change his perspective.

My Husband Moves Back

Rob Bell talks, on his podcast, about when people make big changes in their lives. He says what is often most interesting, is not the point of awakening or change, but all the things that happen next. The fall out, the unfolding, the aftermath. I will agree with Rob Bell, and I will raise him one because when it involves your spouse of sixteen years, the stakes are pretty high.

My husband moved back in February of 2018, and I felt like our life could finally move forward. My awakening had seeped into many areas of my life, and my husband noticed, but the religion piece was the only one that presented a challenge. He was raised in the church, and not only that, but his personality is very black and white, and it lends itself to unwavering commitment. He couldn't fathom, I don't think, that I changed my beliefs about religion, and I no longer believed all the things that I used to believe.

I Wasn't Burned by the Church

I got a question from a family member, asking if I had been burned by the church or found some hypocritical thing that I couldn't get over. Sure, I can give you several examples of when good church people turned their back on couples when talk of divorce started going around. Or when the church commits to work with a ministry in Thailand to help put a stop to human trafficking and walks away when they find out the leaders are two romantically involved women.

Yes, there are plenty of things I could say as to why I *would* leave the church. My reason is not any of those. My reason for leaving the church, and no longer buying into the dogma of original sin and ideas of heaven is because I had evolved. I have transcended and included, meaning I took what I felt was true from the Christian perspective and moved on. I believe Jesus did live, and the Bible has a lot of truths in it for humanity today. End of story.

This will likely sound arrogant to traditional Christians, because I know, I was one. But I believe evolving means you have the expanded consciousness, or bandwidth to think and understand concepts on your own. That gives you the ability to act on your own as well.

When you believe that you are a sinner and that God will judge you when you die, you behave in a certain way. You act like a little child, scared to even ask to go to the bathroom. You don't realize you have the right to make that choice on your own. Well, let me tell you, you do.

Liz Gilbert, said since publishing Eat, Pray, Love, she travels the country writing permission slips for people. It was like they didn't know they could do that, make a choice on their own to choose for themselves. I needed a permission slip, and I gave it to myself. And, if you can't give yourself one, I'm giving you one right now. I give you permission to change your beliefs, decide what is true for you, and not worry about how that information will be received by anyone else.

Judgmental Tendencies

Church people are known for being judgmental, I'm sure this isn't news to you. I didn't go back to church, except for the first Easter after my husband moved back, and that was a mistake. I only went for my kid's sake, and then realized that was confusing for everyone. I wanted to be authentic, not fake it for my kids or the church people.

My husband started going regularly when he moved back, without me, and usually without the kids. I figured that no one would understand my change in beliefs. It was awkward, as I hadn't returned to church with my husband. I assumed everyone from my church was judging me. Whether they were or they weren't, I was assuming they were, and so I felt judged. It's messed up, I realize that. I am only human.

I asked my husband if he felt judged, or uncomfortable going to church alone. He said no, he was fine with it, that it was my choice and not anyone else's business. He's pretty solid like that. I told him I heard that people were saying we were having marital problems because I wasn't there. He said people were going to think whatever they wanted to think. Wow, that's thick skin, I wish I could say the same. I gave too much energy to what people thought, and even though I was confident in my choices and beliefs, it took some time to shake.

Regardless, I didn't return to church. I had nothing to prove and no convincing to do, I just wanted to continue on my path. However, I thought we should probably talk to the kids. They were caught somewhere in the middle of this and as much as we were both conscious of it, we hadn't addressed it.

Talking to the Kids

I wanted to make sure the kids knew why I wasn't going to church, when their dad still was. I also wanted to share my new perspective, so there wasn't any confusion.

The oldest was fourteen, the middle was eleven and the youngest was ten. I wanted them to know what I believed, why it was ok, that it was a choice for them. They didn't have to make the choice right now, but I wanted to share it with them. My husband was fine with that, he seemed to be letting the kids make their own choice, when the time was right. It was still pretty early after my awakening, that it's possible he thought it was a phase I was going through.

We sat them down in our casual living room, near the fireplace. The kids were squirmy, and I don't blame them. I started by sharing with them, simply, what I believed at that moment in time. I didn't believe that we were sinners and Jesus didn't die on the cross for us. It was probably more an explanation of what I didn't believe. I just wanted them to know there were other options, and that it was ok if they had questions or wanted to talk about it. And if not, that was ok, too.

My husband sat quietly while I talked, and then he wanted a turn. Which was odd because the kids, obviously, knew his side since they had been living it their entire lives. Reinforcing all the dogma, God sent his son, Jesus died for you, etc. When he got to the part about hell, the youngest asked if it was really a place that was full of fire. He said yes. And then I interjected.

I recalled an excerpt from Rob Bell's book, *Love Wins: A Book About Heaven, Hell, and the Fate of Every Person Who Ever Lived*. He shares how Hell is not what I was told in church, a place of fire and gnashing of teeth. No, it was a place outside the city where trash was burned in Bible times.

Obviously agitated with me, my husband snapped at me, stating that he didn't interrupt me when I was talking. True, but... I also didn't plan on him going last to reinforce all of his beliefs on the children. The kids already knew what he believed, we had raised them in the church from birth. This didn't feel like we were presenting options and giving them all the choices. Deep breath.

Kids and Church

The kids didn't want to go to church any more

than I wanted to go to church. Part of it was their age and sheer laziness, I was a teen once, I understood. Sometimes they would go, but not often. The girls may go once every couple weeks, and our oldest would only go when I was out of town, which wasn't often.

The kids would come to me and say they don't want to go to church, and I'd ask them why they agreed to go. It seems they felt bad when telling their dad no. He would only talk to the kids when I wasn't around, putting additional pressure on them. I told them, "You have two choices. You can go with your dad, or you can tell him that you don't want to go. He can't make you feel bad, you control how you feel."

I know my husband well enough, after nearly seventeen years of marriage, he was getting them alone and adding a, "I'd really like you to come with me," at the end. This created just enough of a tinge of guilt in a passive aggressive, unconscious shadow, kind of way. We talked about it, and over the course of the next few months things worked themselves out. I think, as with anything, mistakes were made in the beginning and instead of us both feeling confident that the kids could make their own choice, he felt compelled to still try and influence them.

Forcing Our Beliefs on Our Children

When I told my mom about my awakening and how I wouldn't be going to church anymore, she was very understanding. She became a Christian several years after her divorce from my dad, so I wasn't sure how that would go over. I was pleasantly surprised by her response: "God is all-knowing and He must have known this would happen."

She did have one concern, how would my kids know what to believe. She knew the Bible verse, "Train up a child in the way he should go, and when he is old he will not depart from it." (Proverbs 22:6) So if I wasn't telling my kids what to believe, how would they know? I loved this question! As parents we want the best for our children, and often we think our way is the best. We are only human, so I get it.

However, I wanted to model the choices for them, and lead by example, but ultimately, they will choose for themselves. Instead of teaching them how to follow me and my path, I was teaching them self-awareness to eventually make their own choices. My intention was that they would have the confidence to follow their own knowing, and intuition. Also, my kids were all ten and over when we talked to them, so I had a degree of confidence that they had reached a certain level of maturity. They clearly were not mature enough to be the parent or make big life decisions on their own, but old enough to have their own perspective.

That said, we did not confront the kids at any point and make them choose Christianity or not. It wouldn't have been prudent, even though I am sure we both considered it. As parents we came to an agreement, and everything was just fine for a while. It was good until my in-laws tried to intervene and put pressure on my kids to go to church. There is a reason therapists want to know everything about your family of origin... the apple doesn't fall too far from the tree.

This was more than an issue with the kids, obviously, this was a marriage issue. I could list a handful of other things we didn't agree on before I had my awakening, now we didn't have the same value system with which to guide our decision making. How would we ever agree on anything? I am thankful he was open to doing counseling, otherwise, I didn't feel like we would even have the container to have some of these discussions. Since I don't want to get too much into our person life, this will be simply sharing the process and journey I went on.

Couples Counseling

The only way I felt like we could discuss some of these other topics, and maybe get him to understand my point of view, was through therapy. I have done my share of Christian counseling, and I wasn't doing that again. I was going to find an objective, unbiased, non-religious therapist or counselor to navigate this with us.

We went for several months, every two weeks, meeting together with the counselor discussing our marriage and how we navigate these uncharted waters. What I discovered is that I had trouble finding words to describe the concept of awareness, which is a huge part of my awakening. Everything in chapters four through nine in this book had not really gotten solidified. My stage of development at this point was equivalent to a teenager, whereas now, I at least feel like an adult. Not a sage or wise elder yet, but I can explain myself much better now.

I spent too much energy convincing my husband that he had anything in his psyche that needed addressed, and the counselor was no help.

It's like when you feel offended by someone and you bring it to their attention, and instead of getting empathy and an apology, they are condescending and apathetic. They say, "I am sorry you feel that way." Not validating your feelings, accepting any responsibility at all. It was a good time to communicate with my husband, but I would be hard-pressed to say there was any resolution.

The Antagonist

As my journey unfolded, my husband embraced his role as the antagonist in my hero's journey. It is an important position to fill, as the antagonist keeps you on your toes. He came up with that designation for himself so I had to include it, and if you are familiar with Joseph Campbell's Hero's Journey, it was spot on. In many ways he challenged me during this entire journey, but it helped me become who I am today, so it all worked out.

As I was getting ready to publish my book I asked him two things. First, would he like me to change his name, job, or anything in the book, and second, I asked him if he wanted to read my book before it gets published.

With regard to the first question, because of his

line of work, which will not be mentioned in the book, we usually don't put his name on anything public... so that was an easy decision. What I appreciated, but not really, was that he suggested that I change my name. And upon further review, his name has been completely removed, as have the kids names and others who have been included, to protect their identity and privacy.

And about the second question, if he wanted to read my book prior to publishing. I suggested that millions of people would be reading it and I wanted to make sure he was ok with it before I put it out into the world. He didn't seem too concerned, and he has never read any of it. I am sure he has his rationale, but he had his chance, for the record. I think the only thing that may be surprising to him is the connection to my "rock bottom" being about our marriage. When the D.C. assignment didn't bring us closer together, my awakening was largely triggered by that unmet expectation. Anyway, this is my story, so I will move on.

Amy M. Kunkle

11

The Unfolding

Winter is hard, but when the tulips and daffodils start to emerge it seems like heaven on earth. It had been a long winter, and a long eighteen months of this assignment to D.C. and the proverbial spring was finally here. The spring is typically a very busy time for architects. Once the ground thaws, people want to start building and I was busy with work.

I say busy, but I was actually creating my own work. The only way I could really get a design of my own into the world, I thought, was to design and build my own spec home. That's short for speculative, it's what a builder does when he builds a house and then sells it later to someone after it is complete. It takes the scariness of creating something from scratch, like I discussed at the end of chapter four. People have a hard time envisioning what the house could be, so builders have taken it upon themselves take out that step in this situation.

My First Home Design

There is a certain magic that happens when you design a home from scratch, it is like the embodiment of all your hopes and dreams. That may have been a stretch for my first home design, because it wasn't exactly being designed for me, but I was still very excited about it.

I designed a modern, organic style home to be built on the lake property I purchased from my meditation teacher. I was designing a conscious home, which to me meant respectful of the environment, and designed with intention and spiritual connection. The home would be designed just for the site it was to be built on, taking into account views, wind and solar orientation. The home would also feature spaces for solitude, spaces for community and take into account energy and flow of the home.

Since I resigned from my job twelve years ago to

stay home and raise my children, I had never designed an entire home. I achieved my goal of getting licensed as an architect and never got a chance to use it. I am still hoping my idea of Conscious Architecture takes off, but unfortunately, this house was never built. Apparently the banks were very selective when handing out spec loans after the market crash of 2008. I was able to sell my lot to a builder who had started a house on the lot next door, and that would be the end that story.

I still have in my soul the desire to design and build my own home. I had hoped that going to D.C. would set us up to be able to do that, financially. I'm not sure where the miscommunication happened, but it did not. It covered some of our new in-ground pool, and I would tuck away my home design in my file of "unbuilt projects."

The Conscious Perspective

My new favorite word was conscious. I even created an Instagram profile for a time called Conscious Amy. It was a place for me to share about my awakening, concepts that may not be appreciated on my personal profile, and did not seem to fit in on my business page either. I was hiding, plain and simple. It took me a while, almost a year, to merge the accounts on social media! Now I am still wondering if my architecture practice gets revived, will it have a new home on social media? We shall see, until that day, you can always find me on the web at my ever-changing website listed in the resource section.

I felt that considering myself "conscious" was expressing from a point of view that was unbiased, and non-judgmental. If I were to describe it in a more direct way, it is love-centric. To be unbiased and non-judgmental is to look at everything through the eyes of love. Love filters everything that comes into our presence, like rose-colored glasses. Growing up, one of my favorite scripture verses was 1 John 4:18, which begins, "There is no fear in love, but perfect love casts out fear." Fear is living in the past, fear is being scared of the future, fear is doubting our strength and power. Fear is staying stuck in our old ways because it's familiar and comfortable. Fear was the old paradigm, but love is the new one.

We cannot move forward with fear. It can propel us forward, but not consciously. Only love can move us consciously. I invite you to put on rose-colored glasses and look through the eyes of love because it really is better over here.

Not Going Unconscious

The only way I can explain my innate desire to be conscious is by using the opposite as an example. I have gone to great lengths to explain what I think is causing people to be asleep, in programs they didn't choose for themselves. But at the root of it, is the propensity to keep going unconscious. It is the lack of congruence we have between who we ultimately want to be, and our tendencies to be lazy, or unmotivated. It is a real struggle.

I don't pretend to have this figured out. I fall into the trap of showing on Instagram the times I work out and eat healthy, but I don't disclose the weeks I skip exercising and evenings I sit with a bag of potato chips and Heluva dip on my lap. I know I am not alone, or this world wouldn't be in the shape it's in.

I do this with my eating habits all the time, and I'll talk about trying vegetarianism in a minute. I like black and white boundaries, I would rather be on a diet that is no sugar than to constantly exhaust my energy by eating sugar in moderation. There is so much value in discipline, but on a daily basis I don't have it. What I do have is a dream that is bigger than just myself. I want to be better for my kids and for me. So, I bring conscious awareness into everything I do, and when I give up and grab the bag of chips, if that happens, I don't beat myself up over it. The final step, if there is a final step, is compassion. Any awakening, and that includes ones you have every day, will include: awareness, making space, healing and compassion.

Prejudices

Something became very clear to me that we had done wrong in our parenting. It was an unconscious behavior, but that is not an excuse. Being in 'the church' made us draw heavy lines between us and people who didn't look and act like us. To be honest, we raised children like that because we were like that, and it's not an easy thing to admit. I am speaking for myself here, as this is my realization, not my husband's, but I say we because we both raised our children with this conservative Christian viewpoint.

It wasn't until living in D.C. for the year when we even knew people of other races, much less other beliefs. We kept ourselves safe in our suburban, church families, and we never left. Now as an awakened human, and mother, I am trying to help my children see through some of these unconscious beliefs that were instilled in them.

Whether it be ideas of race and religion, or gender, sexuality, even freedom of speech, I was biased, to say the least. All of these topics are heavily programmed in our culture, on both sides of the debate. Millennials are helping to change some of the programming, but it is our own responsibility to have self-awareness and not contribute to the separateness so rampant in our society. We are all one human race, and all a collective consciousness at the root of it. Together we have the power to affect change in the world. John F. Kennedy said, "A rising tide lifts all the boats." And I believe that we really can impact the world together.

Vegetarian Eating

One practice I thought could make the world a better place, and help me have more clarity in my mind and life was to become a vegetarian. I learned, on For the Life of Me podcast with Julie Piatt, that by eating other living beings we would take on their pain and suffering on an energetic level. Not only was factory farmed meat a horrifying existence for animals, but it is destroying the environment.

Since I prepare most of the meals, I decided to sneak in some more vegetarian meals and help my family to eat more vegetables and beans. My family noticed immediately, and I don't think my son will mind me quoting him. He said, "It's ok if you don't go to church anymore, but there is no way we are giving up meat."

Today we are faced with information from every side, even doctors and scientists on both side of every issue, and it's hard to know who to believe. A video by Paul Chek, who is a wise teacher, with many resources online for holistic health and wellness, offered some guidance this dilemma I was facing. Paul suggests asking your soul, or Great Spirit as he sometimes calls God, what your body needs on any given day. He also discusses how people try diets that worked for someone else, and don't examine if they actually work for you. He said that is the behavior of a child, just taking someone else's option for yourself. Paul Chek and the Chek Institute are a great resource for mind, body and soul connection, see the resource section for more information.

I did some soul searching, and I remembered a farm that did an event with my hot yoga studio a few years back. I looked them up and they were exactly what I needed. They sold sustainably raised meats, which means they were so much healthier for you and for the environment. It was a good compromise since my family was not ready to give up meat. It doesn't take much to locate local farms if you are willing to make some effort.

Alcohol

I have used alcohol to self-medicate and numb myself for years. Many of us justify our nightly drink by our desire to unwind or relax for the day, or weekend. I don't fault you, that was me and is in some ways, is still me. I make better choices now, and bring conscious awareness to drinking, but it will always be a struggle if I let it.

The winter I got back from D.C., I gave up alcohol. It was another attempt to have clarity in my mind, clear up negative energy, and not go unconscious, or fall back into unconscious behaviors. I had identified it as a crutch in my life and wanted to release it. I quit for several months, not sure how long exactly, and was fine, but then I started again because it didn't work. Do you ever think you do something for one reason and then it becomes painfully obvious you actually did it for another?

I gave up drinking to be more conscious, and ended up making not drinking into a religion, a dogma that I applied to myself and others. I wasn't comfortable ordering iced tea at a restaurant because I felt judgement from the server when they offered me an alcoholic beverage. They were just doing their job to upsell more expensive drinks, and I was taking it personally and adding additional meaning.

Old habits are hard to break. I'm not talking about drinking, because I could take it or leave it, I'm talking about judging myself and others. It's like the Buddhist sentiment, "Pain is inevitable, suffering is optional." I was adding the suffering to this situation, all the unnecessary thoughts about eating or drinking, that were just not true and not helpful.

Something to Say

This was also the time in my journey that I realized I had something to say, and I wanted to share my story. My first aligned action was to take Rob Bell's online class called *Something to Say*. I also attended a writer's workshop by Hay House Publishing, in Toronto. You may wonder why I'm including this in my book. Maybe it's odd hearing about when I decided to write this book and how I went about doing it. But this too was part of my journey. Having the confidence to even say that out loud was a big step, try it for yourself.

It was the point when I felt with this story stirring inside of me. I have always enjoyed sharing, maybe too much, but I wanted to talk about my awakening and I knew I couldn't just write a social media post about it. I listened to a Robcast episode, and I knew what I had to do. Don't think your soul speaks to you? It does, sometimes we just don't recognize it because it sounds like Rob Bell.

The writer's workshop was a great in person event to kick off my writing journey. Learning all the ins-and-outs of publishing from Hay House helped me get over a lot of the decisions at the beginning of the process. Especially if I was going to self-publish, and how long it takes to traditionally publish, which was too long for me. I entered my original book idea to Hay House in a contest they run for workshop participants, but didn't win. I have been working on my book ever since, and now about fifteen months later, I have it out in the world.

Ignorance is Bliss

I'm not going to pretend that the two plus years covered in this book I was studying, meditating and evolving every second. There will always be ups and downs, some of them intentional, and other not so much. I was running a business, being a mom, in a relationship and trying to work out some pretty big life issues, that can be all consuming in and of itself.

I had my moments of shutting down and ignoring what was going on around me. It is easy when you are on a journey alone to take more time than may be needed, just for the reason that no one else is pushing you. I was going at my own pace, and the important part is that I kept moving. Kept taking small steps in the right direction.

12

Earth School
July -December 2018

I love to travel, and when I went to Toronto, Canada, for the Hay House Writer's Workshop, it reminded me how much I love traveling. Especially internationally, even though Toronto was only about four hours away.

You Only Live Once

I don't know how you take this saying, you only live once, or YOLO as we see all over the internet. I take it very seriously. I would even consider adding it to my gravestone, FYI family.

Think that's morbid? At least I've thought about it. Gary Vaynerchuk says that the best advice he's ever given is that we only have one life. It's powerful if you let it sink in. Don't let the superficiality of social media down play this idea, this is real wisdom.

My daughters were ten and eleven, and at the perfect age, in my opinion to get exposure to another country. As much as my husband traveled, he wasn't interested in going and so I made it a girls trip, which made Paris the perfect destination. Besides, I took my son to Toronto, the girls got to have a trip. That's fair, right?

When I was in college I went on a trip to several cities and countries in Europe as part of the architecture and landscape architecture program. The instructor had his two kids along, and they were around ten or twelve years old. I remember feeling, even as a twenty-four year old, that I want to do the same type of thing with my kids. For some reason, people my parent's age seemed to be skittish of international travel. I am glad I'm not like that, there are too many amazing places in the world to see.

So many people plan elaborate vacations for when their kids graduate from high school, or when they celebrate their 40th wedding anniversary. That's not me. I know how much a plane ticket to Paris is, and it wasn't going to break the bank. We didn't just go to Europe, we made memories that will bond us forever. I was able to capture a moment in my daughters' lives that I may not have gotten if they were eighteen or older. You can never get that time back.

Underestimating our Youth

The girls and I love macarons, and love baking. I have baked with them since they could reach the counter standing on a chair. By this time, the younger one could roll out pizza dough better than anyone I knew, and the older one could separate eggs like a pro. I decided to sign us up for an advanced macaron cooking class when we were in Paris.

The class was designed for adults, it was not a kids class, by any stretch of the imagination. I emailed ahead to make sure they could participate, explaining their competency level. However, something must have gotten lost in translation because the head chef greeted us at the door, but then quickly went back into the kitchen. A moment later a man comes out and tells us that we wouldn't be able to participate because the class is so fast paced that the children would never be able to keep up. They hadn't met *my* children.

I explained that both of the girls had ample experience baking, but I agreed to forego my spot and "help" the younger one. They begrudgingly let us in, and I don't have to tell you what happened, I think you know. The girls not only held their own, they killed it. The other class participants were tourists, with little to no baking experience. They never had a shot against the Kunkle women.

Whenever my kids want to learn how to do something, they go to YouTube. Sure, I teach them a lot, but the amount of information at their fingertips is beyond any that has been available before. At this point in time, our children really are the future. I believe the kids of the world are going to pass up the level of consciousness of many of the adults in the world. Thanks to them, we have a chance to turn things around on the planet. No pressure parents, but really, wake up.

Authoritative Parenting

I was so intrigued by looking at parenting differently, and read the *Conscious Parent* and *Awakened Family* books, by Dr. Shefali Tsabary. I also heard her speak at the Summit of Greatness

Conference this past year. It made so much sense to me that our children are here to walk their own path and not be a carbon copy of me or my husband. It made a huge difference in my mindset around parenting, and will continue to as I evolve and as they evolve.

As a conservative Christian, parents were the authority figures. In our home there was a clear hierarchy, husband, wife, then kids and our power came from God. When raising our kids in the church, I felt like we didn't have much "why" in our discipline or backing to our beliefs. We took a position that we were older, wiser and stronger than the kids. It was an authoritarian monarchy just like our religion was. Remember my kids are older now, so I'm referring to children over the age of ten.

I now know, post-awakening, that they are here to have their own experience. We are here to show them the importance of being true to themselves by embodying what they value. We are creating a container in which they can hopefully grow and evolve and become healthy, contributing adults. One way we can model this for them is to live it ourselves. Show them how to think for themselves, and how you do the same.

It can be scary as parents to give children what

sounds like a lot of freedom. First, I am not talking about young children. I am referring to my own kids who are preteen and teenagers, and have most of their personality and identity formed. And second, they have always been free, they are not our possessions. When they gain the confidence to make their own choices, not just choosing our beliefs, or the choices of the collective from culture and society, we know we are getting there. We are raising sentient beings, not robots.

Awareness with Kids

One evening after dinner my fifteen-year-old son, went to his room to complete a homework assignment. After he finished, he sat down next to me on the couch. He said he thought it was the best assignment he's turned in this year. I said, "explain," which is something I say to get my kids to talk freely.

He said the assignment was to read a story and write a paragraph in response to it. This was the third such assignment, but the first he actually felt good about. The first time he completed it, he said he forgot about it, so his friend had to tell him what the story was about and he wrote a response that way. The second story he skimmed over in study hall, where there were a lot of distractions and he wrote his response then. The third one he did in his room, just then, after he read the whole story and immediately wrote the response.

It was as if a lightbulb went on for him, even though it was just a homework assignment. He said he felt like he was able to understand it better, and in turn, wrote a better response. I thought that was so great for him to observe his situation and the various outcomes of his decisions, and then consciously take action to get a better result. This is conscious awareness in action.

The Marriage Dynamic

It is probably pretty apparent by now that my husband and I are in opposition as it relates to our value systems. I admit, I changed, and he didn't, so I take full responsibility for the dissonance that I brought into our marriage. Most things that we discussed, I now had a different perspective. It was tense at times, as you can imagine.

When we got married, we were on the same page. We met at a Baptist church in Tucson, Arizona. I was in my last year of college and he was on his first assignment with the military. At that time our value systems matched, our personalities were very different, but that was ok. What probably wasn't ok was how different our goals in life were. Maybe twenty years ago, if I had listened to him say that he wanted a family, and he had listened to me when I said I wanted a career, we would be in very different places in life now. Our pre-marital counseling intake quiz showed that we were both naïve and overly optimistic about our future life together. That happens at twenty-five, and I don't regret one minute of it. Everything happens for our growth and evolution. However, I would have some very different advice to my twenty-five year old self.

Back then, I had the feeling that we would change in our life, it seemed normal to me, change seemed normal. However, I thought that we would change together. That we would be traveling on this path of life together and we would change and grow together. But that's not how it happened, somewhere along the journey we started walking alone. I changed and he didn't.

He was *ok* with my decision to choose a different path, but he wasn't going to change, so it was settled, we would stay on different paths. I wanted to be cognizant of how the kids were faring in all of this change, but they seemed very resilient. I was still a little unsure where they would land on some of the issues their father and I didn't agree on. So, I had this this conversation with my husband about how to dissolve our preferences and love them unconditionally.

Preference and Judgement

I talked about prejudices earlier, and this goes hand in hand with that. In the Christian religion, there were a lot of things viewed as wrong like pre-marital sex, divorce, and homosexuality. These were some of the topics in which my perspective had changed because I became open to taking in more information and perspectives about these things. I have seen situations where kids grow up and feel like they don't live up to their parents expectations, and as a result, there is a loss of relationship.

As a parent, if we have a preference or opinion over something in our children's lives, we set that as a standard they have to live up to. For example, if we think that our children should not be gay, that only dating or marrying someone of the opposite sex is ok, that sets a standard for our children. Our standard, not theirs. Our preference, not necessarily theirs.

If we tell them, we will not 'like' that decision,

but will love them anyway, our preference still looms over their choice. I have heard that statement so many times in the Christian church. It's almost as if the parent wants to absolve themselves for the poor decision of their child. The problem that I see happening in that situation is that our children will always feel like they don't measure up to our standard. We can say we love them all day long, but they will always feel that standard is preventing their parent(s) from loving and supporting them unconditionally. They won't feel loved, the judgement, how we perceive their choice, blocks the connection to the child.

What is the solution? Dissolve the preference. We can't have a preference over what we want them to be. We just have to truly accept and support what they feel is right. This happens by releasing our attachment to their outcome, as in I am ok either way with their choice. I want my children to feel our unconditional love and acceptance no matter how their lives unfold. What if we could raise children that didn't need our approval?

Children Who Don't Need our Approval

Wow, what a concept. I see this a lot in my friends with older children, and even in adults who are still seeking their parents approval. The kids, even after they have left home still need their parents approval because the parents failed to successfully release their child into the world. I believe it's called cutting the apron strings, which I think refers more to the mother's attachment, but it is valid for both parents. A sign of a well-parented child is one who is independent and so confident in themselves that they don't need our approval.

If you haven't healed your own shadow or pain-body, it's like piling boxes into your basement. When you pass away, your children will have to go through the boxes of junk you have stored in there. They don't want to do that, and you don't want to put that responsibility on them. Unconscious parents hold onto all their junk filled boxes, and their children have to clean up what's left after they're gone. The unfortunate part is that the children have boxes of their own to deal with.

You have one chance to parent your children, and this is it. No one said it was going to be easy, in fact, if you asked anyone they probably said it is the most challenging thing you could do in life. But I will say, as true as that is, it has also been the most fulfilling aspect of my life. They have taught me so much and have shown me just how much love my heart can hold.

13

Presence

Eckhart Tolle defines presence as consciousness without thought. I realize now, if we can be aware and not judge, or have thoughts about our awareness, we are at peace. A concept that took me a while to understand was how to actually live in the present moment. Eckhart Tolle points out, and maybe others have before him, that we only have this moment. The past is truly only alive in our memories, and the future is something that has not happened yet. I was living my life, day by day in excited anticipation to see what unfolded.

Meeting Jess Lively

In September of 2018 I attended a live workshop Jess Lively did in Detroit, Michigan, of all places! Just three hours from me, and what a fun city that has gone through some major transformation of its own. I absolutely love live events, and meeting Jess in person was surreal. Podcasts have a way of making you feel like you know the person on the other end of the microphone, it's weird.

The event was part workshop and part group coaching, and I signed up to do one-on-one inner voice work with her. If you want to hear it, Jess gave me permission to air the session on my Amy Kunkle Audio Hour podcast, Episode 15.

Jess reminded me of the second book that Eckhart Tolle wrote, *A New Earth, Awakening to Your Life's Purpose*. How did I miss that subtitle? I read The Power of Now early on and I didn't pick up the next book because I was not in a place spiritually to grasp much of the book the first time through. I didn't read *A New Earth* until Jess talked about it at the workshop. Now that I've read it, I consider it my practical guide to conscious living. It is never very far from my reach. Eckhart Tolle teaches a way of being, not what to believe, like religion does.

I should have known Jess Lively would be instrumental in yet another of my life changes because that is how the Universe works. I also met other like-minded people who also have been following along on her journey. My inner voice session with Jess came at a perfect time in my journey, shocking, I know.

My Inner Voice Work

Jess had shared more about Spiral Dynamics during the weekend and my mind was reeling a bit. I talk about Spiral Dynamics in the introduction, but briefly since that was thirteen chapters ago, it is a framework for human development, as it relates specifically to our value systems. It was as if I was able to see my growth over the past two years, and somehow validate it with this model.

However, it also created the judgement and comparison, which I was trying to avoid. I wanted to talk with Jess, in my one-on-one session, about how you function in the world knowing this information. How do I live in the higher state of consciousness with others, very close to me, in a less evolved state. I know this is sounding judgmental, but stick with me.

During the inner voice work, Jess helps you

"tap into" your intuition or your own deeper wisdom. It is like getting into a state of meditation with deep breath and focused attention, and is basically channeling your higher self. In my inner voice work with Jess, she helped me to see that I was still approaching many areas of my life from lower states of consciousness, out of habit.

I became aware that I was making a "religion" out of the freedom that I now felt. I had been making rules, in my mind, out of how I thought people around me should be living, and I imposed my belief system on them. I was applying my old authoritative, rules-based system to myself and the people around me now, instead of truly coming from a place of love, acceptance and allowing.

As our session wrapped up, I was reminded that everyone can still have their own experience. And that it's not my job to ensure anyone else spirals up the spiral of evolution in this lifetime. Even my kids and even my husband. Just like you can't change them, you can't save them, and you can evolve them. You can only change yourself.

Messages from the Unconscious

Nearly a year later, when I was publishing this book, I had a dream that brings this concept together. It was almost as if my unconscious mind was reminding me that I can't change anyone else.

Carl Jung said dreams emerge from the unconscious as symbols and messages from our unconscious mind. His theories on dream interpretation suggest that dreams are doing the work of integrating our conscious and unconscious lives. This was exciting!

In my dream I was diving in the ocean with friends, one of which I recognized as Aubrey Marcus, podcaster and influencer that I follow. I am not a great swimmer, especially in the ocean, so the important part here is that I am doing something that in real life has triggered panic attacks and is really scary for me. But, in my dream, I ease through it and pop back up to the surface.

I look around, then turn to Aubrey and ask where the other two people are. We are diving with two other people, women I think, and they had not come back up yet. I think he said this, or I had this overall feeling of comfort, that no matter what happened, the other two were here to have their own experience. Everyone is supposed to have their own experience. And then I woke up.

After meditating on this dream, I realized that the people who went in the water and didn't come back up may have died. My realization is that they chose that experience. It was very stirring to consider that something even as drastic as someone dying could be ok, but I understood. Message heard loud and clear.

Awakening to my Life's Purpose

After the weekend in Detroit, I took time to read *A New Earth, Awakening to Your Life's Purpose*, by Eckhart Tolle. We think our life's purpose is a big deal, but really it's not. That idea is something our culture has convinced us is true, its hidden in the subliminal messaging from our culture. Feeling like you have something major to accomplish just keeps us living in a state of anxiety, in the future and not in the present moment.

Our purpose is how we express in the world, and when we have done the work to awaken spiritually, it will likely be connected to our deeper

Self. I believe I found my purpose this way. I believe my purpose is connected to why I'm writing this book, and maybe it involves architecture or parenting, I'm not too worried about it. As I look at my life over the past twenty years, how things have unfolded, I realize that I have found my purpose along my path. If you aren't worried about what you are going to do, you just follow the path and eventually your purpose will emerge.

Merging my Life

I had gone through so much change internally the past two years, and it obviously affected every area of my life. Some of the changes were integrated as I went along, others needed more time to merge. This awakening started me on a lifelong journey to wholeness, not one that could be completed in two years.

Conscious parenting, eating, drinking, exercise, and meditation were all practices I was using to create the life I wanted. The areas of my life that still needed resolution were my career and my marriage. I don't know if either will have any true resolution, but I'll wrap them up for this book anyway.

These have been the areas of my life that were rooted the deepest in my old program, which explains why it has taken more time to align them with my new way of being.

Career Alignment

I wanted to be an architect from the time I was in eighth grade, and pursued it with determination until I earned my licensed in 2006 in California, then Ohio later. I had been licensed for over ten years when I started Amy Kunkle Creative, Conscious Architecture, in the summer of 2017, but had never practiced on my own. As I say with anything, you have to start down the path to see if it's right for you.

And then, true to my awakening, I was able to look at my career differently. I see my purpose, which I believe is sharing my awakening journey, possibly merge with my architectural practice. Ultimately that is why I created "Conscious Architecture" in the first place. Call it a synchronicity, a sign from the Universe, or God, letting me know I am on the right path.

If someday I am able to do conscious architecture and spiritually connected design, it will be a wonderful expression of my life. If I can travel the world and share insight from my spiritual awakening, it too will be a wonderful unfolding.

Relationship Alignment

All the other areas of my life don't involve another human as much as this one. And that's the thing about marriage, you are in it together. At least that is how the story goes, how the program from our western society runs. Until death do you part runs on repeat, all the while we have countless marriages disconnected and unhealthy.

As our culture evolves, we may not think so much of getting married in the traditional sense, but in what areas of your life you want a partner. I will be honest, my views even on marriage have changed. Especially how I will talk to my children about it as they grow up. Neither the Disney fairytale, nor a conservative Christian view will be teaching my kids how to choose someone to join them on this journey of life and love.

My husband and I have been married for seventeen years, and we will be ok. We have gone through a lot in our marriage, and in many ways this was an awakening for our relationship. Now we will have to decide if we use this opportunity to grow and thrive together, or separately. I am not attached to the outcome, it will be what it will be. However, I won't be able to tell you what happens, simply because I don't know at this point, maybe another book down the road.

The Hero's Journey

Joseph Campbell created what is called the Hero's Journey, a template for transformation describing a hero and an adventure he or she goes on. It's a common theme adopted by Hollywood as part of any good movie. Your Hero's Journey could be an awakening, like mine, a short journey like Dorothy's in The Wizard of Oz, or a lifetime like Luke Skywalker in Star Wars.

There is value to every part of the journey, the call to adventure, the ordeal, the road back, but the most important part is the last part, where the hero brings the "elixir" back to the ordinary world. If you don't make it to this point, you probably haven't learned the lesson you were supposed to learn along the way. Every time you have awareness in a situation, you can choose to make space in your life for expansion. You can heal your unconscious or programmed beliefs and become whole. And you can have compassion for yourself when you don't.

14

No Really, What do I do Now?

It doesn't seem fair to leave you hanging if you are also on this path. The choice to leave the known, the comfortable, can be tough. It means we may not live up to our parents expectations. It means we might let down our youth pastor or our godparents. It means we may be alone because everyone else stayed behind. I'm not going to lie to you. If you choose freedom, it is at a cost, but well worth it.

But you deserve this. You deserve to be free, inside and out. There isn't anyone else in this world that gets to tell you how to think, feel and live. You get to, and if you don't know how to figure things out on your own, I'll get you started. You don't have to follow my path, and you surely don't have to believe what I believe. You simply need to loosen the grip of what has been holding you down and find the truth that is in you.

This doesn't work if you just accept what I'm telling you as your new way to be. You have to do some of the work on your own. You have to turn inward, in the stillness and discover your own truth. Consider what isn't working in your life even though you pretend it is. Look at your belief system and be honest with yourself, why does it feel so empty. It will always have the feeling of lack when it doesn't come from inside you, from your soul.

Awakenings

You can either choose to do the work, or you will find yourself in the midst of a God, or Universe, orchestrated life-changing event. It's the man who has a heart attack and almost loses everything, or the woman who has a stroke and that makes her slow down and realize the gift of life she has been given. If you need a wake-up call, the Universe will provide it. I would suggest not letting it come to that. I am here to help you with whatever awakening you are going through, big or small.

In order to allow this awakening go deeper than the superficial ramifications of something like a mid-life crisis, you have to consciously connect it to your soul. Often as children we have no trouble connecting to our true nature, happy and carefree. But then at some point because of our program, family, culture or trauma we lose that connection. We disconnect.

If you're awakening was health related, you will have the natural tendency to just treat the symptoms. Instead, seek to solve the root of the problem from a place of the mind and thoughts, connect it to deeper truths. Feel into the root cause. Was the Universe trying to tell you something? When we change the perspective from something happening to you, to something happening for you, we can learn the lesson.

Here are my four steps for navigating any awakening in your life. They will give you simple direction for doing the work on your own. They can also help you to approach your life in a conscious, holistic way. You can use each step by itself, or you can use them together, however they are needed in your life. Please stay open at each step to listen to your own intuition.

STEP ONE

Awareness

Observe your thoughts and actions, objectively, like when I described vlogging. You are looking through the camera at your life, not just staying inside your mind. There are a lot of terms used for this, the watcher, the observer, even mindfulness because that refers to being conscious of something.

I also use the term present moment awareness because you can only have awareness in the present moment. If you are thinking about your past, or a mistake you made yesterday, you aren't having awareness. You are creating confusion for your mind. Let's say you snapped at your child yesterday, and you want to think about it for a moment so you can learn from the mistake. The moment is already in the past, the damage has been done, and by giving your energy to that past mistake you are taking presence away from today.

Another practical way to have awareness is to take the mind identified "labels" off of things. Eckhart Tolle uses this example often when he describes finding stillness in nature. Try taking a walk and looking around at flowers and trees and not letting your mind name them. I imagine like in

Sesame Street, or Dora the Explorer children's cartoons, when a new object comes on the screen and a little box shows up with the name for that object. This is what your brain has a tendency to do, but you can give your brain a rest and connect to your other senses. Take in the color, smell and touch of something. How does it feel and what feelings does it evoke?

Awareness can at first be shining a flashlight on your internal life, and then reflect into your outer world to bring consciousness to your entire life.

STEP TWO

Making Space

The process of making space takes place in every segment of our life. I am ultra-practical. So, here is some practical guidance on how to apply this concept of making space in your life, and not get sucked back into the Matrix. I refer to life often as a hamster wheel. You unconsciously get on and just keep going in circles.

If there is no room for growth, then growth will not occur, or it will be painful when it does. Just like a river forcing its way through an embankment, if growth is inevitable then it will make a way.

Making space in our minds can occur in a few different ways. First of all, giving yourself time each day where it can turn the thoughts off and be quiet. Many people wonder why they have trouble falling asleep at night, but what happens is that time is the only quiet your mind has had all day. Its ok to use that time to meditate, and let the thoughts go, as long as you aren't battling yourself and your desire to actually be sleeping.

Second, our minds stay active with thoughts when we aren't disciplined in how we think. I am often exhausted by people that ruminate on issues for days. It's a waste of energy and is a misuse of your time. If you need to make a decision, make it right then, and if you don't need to make it yet or don't have all the information, then stop thinking about it. By helping our mind to differentiate if and when we need to be thinking, we can clear out excess mind clutter.

Third and lastly, build time into your week, month or year to enjoy quiet time and disconnect from the grind of daily life. Vacations are not enough, you need an afternoon once a week or a day each month to just be. When you don't schedule the time, it gets taken by other things. When you fill your vacation with activities, you don't get the break you need. Take a walk without earbuds or a podcast playing, it can be that simple.

STEP THREE

Healing

How do you uncover something in the depths of your unconscious? Chances are, it's coming out in what bothers you about someone else. Carl Jung says our shadow often shows up in projection, meaning you may accuse your partner of something that is actually present in you. For example, I could tell my husband he is too tight fisted with money when all the while I am the one who feels the lack of resources. Another example, I may point out that my sister has bad eating habits, when what is really going on is I am struggling with food.

There are a number of ways to discover what needs to be healed, and then simply bringing it into your awareness is most of the work. Knowledge is potential power, says Napoleon Hill. It is potential power because you still have to do something about it. Knowing what you need to heal isn't doing you any good if you aren't willing to organize or analyze the information in order to heal.

Jess Lively says, on her podcast, that you don't need to pay a coach or someone outside of yourself to figure these things out. You just need to tap into your own inner knowing. Throughout this book, especially in the chapter titled Healing the Unconscious, I discuss modalities of healing if you want to try something else. I enjoy Reiki and saying positive affirmations, amongst other things. Don't add judgement to the process, if you like talk therapy do it. If you like Reiki Energy Healing, do that. Find healing practices that you enjoy and do those.

STEP FOUR

Compassion

You have a divine purpose here on the planet, and it is in that realization that you will find the strength to live your life in alignment with your values. But we are human and the stressors of our life can take over, without realizing it. And that's ok. That is the moment when you love yourself more.

I have the best of intentions to exercise and eat healthy, but sometimes I just don't make time. The best way I can respond to myself in that situation is to have gratitude for what I am making time for, and next time, be aware of how I am aligning my priorities. Just like when I discussed present moment awareness, there is zero value in brooding over the past. If you feel amazing when you take time to work out, then you will take time to work out. Until then, work on a painting or spend time with your kids.

Spiritual Bypass

I like talking about spiritual topics as much as the next soulpreneur, have you heard that term? It is soul + entrepreneur, for those of you that missed it. I love all the talk of mystical, spirit filled lives online and in real life, but I am just as leery of becoming consumed with doing things that are good for you as much as doing things that aren't.

Spiritual bypass is the idea that we are just replacing our old non-spiritual habit with a new spiritual habit and not being conscious in the moment. Paying attention to what we are doing in the first place will help, and asking ourselves why we start something or why we become complacent with the practice over time. If it's not serving you, let it go.

An example of spiritual bypass is to do something like meditation or grounding and make a discipline out of it, doing it unconsciously like you would watch tv. Checking something off your list is a task the ego or persona would do, to gratify itself. Bring conscious awareness to everything you do and you won't get caught in spiritual bypass.

By applying one or all of my four principles of awakening you won't get stuck in a practice that goes unconscious.

Your journey

There are many people waking up in the world today, for many reasons, and you may be one of them. Some days it feels like the earth is buzzing with new, vibrant energy. And it is, that's us! The one we are waiting for is here. Julie Piatt, or SriMati, her mystical mother name, says, "You are the one you are waiting for. The divine emanation of you is the one that will save you if you need saving."

The good news is, the world is waking up and evolving, but it has been a slow process, collectively. Eckhart Tolle wrote the two books I refer to in this book, in 1997 and 2005. However, because of the internet we are now hitting a time of exponential growth. We see the strongholds of government and religion start to loosen, and people everywhere are becoming empowered by their own truth.

Let my awakening guide you. Rewrite the narrative of your future, based on your own truth.

Much love + namaste!

Amy M. Kunkle

15

Epilogue
January -July 2019

Hello my new friend! Thank you for being here. This was new for me, this writing a book *thing*. It has been a challenge, and an adventure into the unknown. This book and my message is my elixir for you to use now to go on your own journey. I appreciated every minute of it and I hope you do, too.

Around the two year mark, my awakening experience had come to fruition, it was December 2016-December 2018, almost to the day. I think it's important to point that out because I want to move on to the next thing. As much as I loved this journey of awakening, I am ready for the next one. I have continued to change and explore more fun things that I didn't talk about in this book simply because there wasn't enough *space* for it. Not just space on the page, but also mental capacity...I didn't want to overwhelm either of us with too much information.

Writing this book was a healing modality of its own for me. It was one thing to experience the awakening in real life, and it was a whole different thing to put that experience into words. I learned so much about myself and the process of writing that I am sure I could teach at least one class on it... said by a true entrepreneur. I would like to keep writing books, and I am also hoping to do more soul connected, conscious architecture.

The one thing I would like to close with as it was a bit of a confirmation from the Universe, or God, in a way, that I am on the right path. Though not necessary, it's nice to feel validation in some way. My wink from the Universe came by way of an astrology reading. Now, if you've been with me this long, to be through my entire book, I am pretty sure you're going to be ok with me sharing how an astrologist was involved. Let's find out, shall we?

An astrology reading is done using the date and time of birth, because you are unique, and it's a scientific representation of history. My astrology reading, of my Natal chart for those of you who know what I'm talking about, shows the overall picture of my entire life. When I was sitting with the astrologist, she immediately asked what happened two and a half years ago. It pointed exactly to my December 2016 awakening experience. She said I responded to the obvious prompting of my soul to follow this path. She also said I am stepping into my life's purpose by writing this book. She showed me where my chart reveals that I was destined to be a spiritual teacher. I wasn't sure if I should laugh or cry, I picked both.

I immediately wondered how architecture would truly mesh with being a spiritual teacher. And she advised me this: Embrace your path. I took that as, all is well. I don't need to take one over the other, I will embrace them both and appreciate all the life experience I have had thus far.

I am excited to continue to integrate and grow more in my parenting and family life. I will forever love learning and intend to share along the way. I may be trying some in-person classes and events, so check my website for information. I'll be doing book related events in the summer and fall of 2019, after that, you'll just have to follow me online to keep up with where I am and what I'm doing.

Thank you again for your support in purchasing and reading this book, I am forever grateful to you.

Namaste, Amy

Resources

My YouTube Channel:

Amy Kunkle (I have two, it's not the one with paper crafting tutorials, it is the one with the VLOGS and self-awareness videos)

Summit of Greatness 2017 Conference: VLOG 048

Podcast: Amy Kunkle Audio Hour

Website: www.amykunkle.com

Facebook: Amy Kunkle

Instagram: Amy.Kunkle.Creative

Podcasts I like or refer to:

The Lively Show, Jess Lively

Episode 185, *The intersection of rational mind and intuitive guidance with Erin Loechner*

Episode 242, *Exploring consciousness & healing eyesight naturally with Jacob Lieberman*

Good Life Project, Jonathan Fields

Art of Charm, Jordan Harbinger (at that time)

The School of Greatness, with Lewis Howes

Robcast, Rob Bell

Rich Roll Podcast

For the Life of Me, Julie Piatt

The GaryVee Audio Experience

Aubrey Marcus Podcast

Living 4D with Paul Chek

This Jungian Life

Under the Skin, Russel Brand

Books I recommend in chronological order of when I read them:

2015

Cameron, Julia (2002) *The Artist's Way: A Spiritual Path to Higher Creativity.* New York: Penguin Putnam Inc.

McKeown, Greg (2014) *Essentialism: The Disciplined Pursuit of Less.* Virgin Books

2016

Cardone, Grant (2012) *10X Rule: The Only Difference Between Success and Failure.* Wiley

Hill, Napoleon (2016, First Edition: 1937) *Think and*

Grow Rich. Sound Wisdom

Flynn, Pat (2016) *Will it Fly? How to Test Your Next Business Idea So You Don't Waste Your Time and Money.* Flynndustries, LLC

Sinek, Simon (2011) *Start with Why: How Great Leaders Inspire Everyone to Take Action.* Portfolio

Kaufman, Scott Barry and Gregorie, Carolyn (2016) *Wired to Create: Unraveling the Mysteries of the Creative Mind.* TarcherPerigee

Elrod, Hal (2012) *The Miracle Morning: The Not-So-Obvious Secret Guaranteed to Transform Your Life – (Before 8AM).* Hal Elrod

Howes, Lewis (2017) *The School of Greatness: A Real-World Guide to Living Bigger, Loving Deeper, and Leaving a Legacy.* Rodale Books

2017

Robbins, Tony (2017) *Unshakeable: Your Financial Freedom Playbook.* Simon & Schuster

Tolle, Eckhart (2004) *The Power of Now: A Guide to Spiritual Enlightenment.* Namaste Publishing

Wright, Frank Lloyd (1957) *A Testament.* Bramhall House

Yogananda, Paramahansa (1998) *Autobiography of a*

Yogi (Self-Realization Fellowship). Self-Realization Fellowship

Haanel, Charles (2010) *The Complete Master Key System*. Snowball Publishing

Pirsig, Robert M. (2005) *Zen and the Art of Motorcycle Maintenance: An Inquiry Into Values*. William Morrow Paperbacks

2018

Zukav, Gary (2014) *The Seat of the Soul: 25th Anniversary Edition*. Simon & Schuster

Bernstein, Gabrielle (2018) *The Universe Has Your Back: Transform Fear into Faith*. Hay House

Bell, Rob (2012) *Love Wins: A Book About Heaven, Hell, and the Fate of Every Person Who Ever Lived*. HarperOne

Tsabary PhD, Shefali (2010) *The Conscious Parent: Transforming Ourselves, Empowering Our Children*. Namaste Publishing

Dispenza, Dr. Joe (2017) *Becoming Supernatural: How Common People Are Doing the Uncommon*. Hay House

Singer, Michael A. (2007) *The Untethered Soul: The Journey Beyond Yourself*. New Harbinger Publications

Fields, Jonathan (2018) *How to Live a Good Life: Soulful Stories, Surprising Science, and Practical Wisdom.* Hay House

Carnegie, Dale (1998) *How to Win Friends & Influence People.* Pocket Books

Tolle, Eckhart (2016) *A New Earth: Awakening to Your Life's Purpose.* Penguin Books

Hawkins MD. PhD, David (2014) *Letting Go: The Pathway to Surrender.* Hay House Inc.

Tsabary PhD, Shefali (2017) *The Awakened Family: How to Raise Empowered, Resilient, and Conscious Children.* Penguin Books

Singer, Michael A. (2015) *The Surrender Experiment: My Journey into Life's Perfection.* Harmony

Selig, Paul (2018) *The Book of Freedom (Mastery Trilogy/Paul Selig Series).* TarcherPerigee

Amy M. Kunkle

ABOUT THE AUTHOR

Amy Kunkle is an architect, wife and mother. She lives
in Canton, Ohio and enjoys meditation, spending time
with her family, reading and taking walks with her
dog, Buckeye.

You can follow Amy on Instagram and
Facebook or visit her website:

www.amykunkle.com

Made in the USA
Columbia, SC
18 September 2019